Lost Termini of North West England

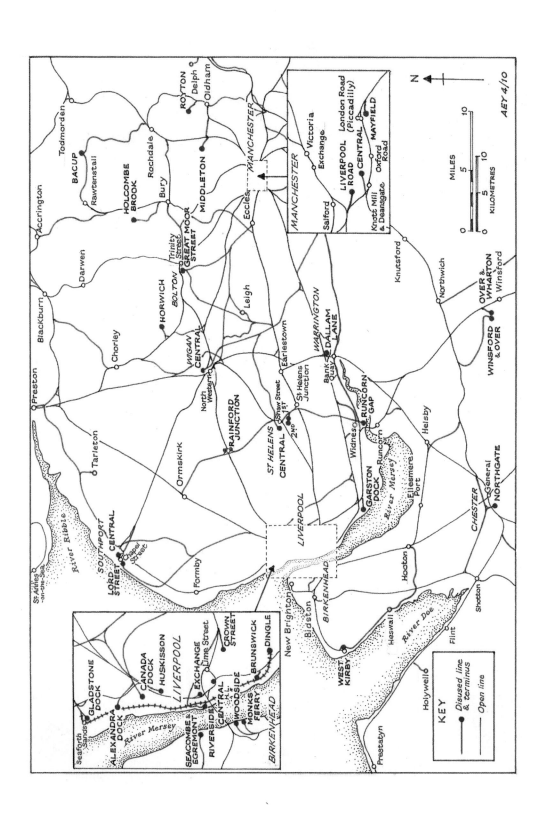

Lost Termini of
North West England

Paul Wright

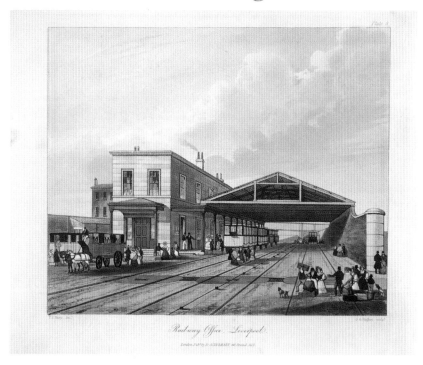

Railway Office, Liverpool

Silver Link Publishing Ltd

First published in 2010

British Library Cataloguing in Publication Data

A catalogue record for this book is available from the British Library.

ISBN 978 1 85794 316 0

Title page: **Liverpool Crown Street:** A print from 1831 by the artist Thomas Berry shows a view of Crown Street Station looking towards the east. *Thomas Berry*

Silver Link Publishing Ltd
The Trundle
Ringstead Road
Great Addington
Kettering
Northants NN14 4BW

Tel/Fax: 01536 330588
email: sales@nostalgiacollection.com
Website: www.nostalgiacollection.com

Printed and bound in the Czech Republic

Please note:
Silver Link Publishing Ltd (Silver Link) is not responsible for the content of external websites. The reasons for this are as follows:

Silver Link does not produce them or maintain/update them and cannot change them.
Such sites can be changed without Silver Link's knowledge or agreement.

Where external links are given they may be to websites which also offer commercial services, such as online purchasing. The inclusion of a link or links to a website(s) in our books should not be taken or understood to be an endorsement of any kind of that website(s) or the site's owners, their products or services.

Dedication

Dedicated to the memory of my late Grandfather William Boardman who awakened my interest in closed stations by taking me to see several, during informative and happy walks, around the decaying parts of Liverpool in the 1970s.

The Author - Paul Wright

The author was born in Wallasey in 1964 into a Liverpool family. His childhood coincided with a sharp decline in the fortunes of Britain's railways. In 1965 the he moved to Widnes, a small industrial town that could once boast eight active passenger stations, two of which were within a short walk of the author's home. With regular Saturday and school holiday visits to Grandparents in the Walton area of Liverpool there were plenty of railway locations where the author could play and explore during the 1970s and this awakened a fascination in the subject.

Since 1986 the Paul has enjoyed a career in Local Government working within Public Parks, currently being employed by Halton Borough Council as the head of their Open Space Services. Interestingly the he now has responsibility for many of the former railway sites on which he used to play as they have over the years been developed as public open spaces.

In 1989 the author moved back to Wallasey and since 1991 he has been a serving Crew Member with the RNLI's New Brighton Station and currently holds the rank of Hovercraft Commander.

In 2005 the Paul discovered Nick Catford's Closed Stations Website and sent in some of his material for inclusion. The result was that the he became a contributor to the site concentrating on the North West and North Wales area. Since 2005 he has contributed material for hundreds of stations that are now on the website.

Paul is also a keen motorcyclist, enjoys music, cinema, running and the study of his family history.

Contents

Acknowledgements

Thanks to Nick Catford for starting the Closed Stations Website, which has become such a popular railway history site and which has led to the publication of this book. Thanks also to Nick for the help that he gave me especially in preparing the maps and photographs.
Thanks to Bevan Price for making available for my use his large collection of North West area photographs and for helping me to carry out the site surveys. Without Bevan's help the process would have taken much longer.

Thank you to Michael Stewart for providing access to his extensive ticket collection, many of which appear in this book.

Thanks to Alan Young for drawing the area map and thank you to Peter Townsend of Silver Link Publishing for encouraging the idea of a companion book to the Website.

The Ordnance Survey deserve a special mention as without their fine products, both past and present, the survey work and presentation of closed station information, both on the website and in the book, would not have the clarity that it does.

And thank you to all of those many people who have helped me in a variety of ways including the current owners of closed stations who gave me access to their property.

Bibliography

An Illustrated History of the Cheshire Lines Committee by Paul Bolger *Heydey Publishing*

An Illustrated History of Liverpool's Railways by Paul Anderson *Irwell Press*

An Illustrated Survey of Liverpool's Railway Stations 1830 – 1985 by Rob Gell *Heyday Publishing*

An Illustrated Survey of Railway Stations between Southport and Liverpool 1848 – 1986 by Rob Gell *Heyday Publishing*

British Railway Atlas 1955 Ian Allan

British Railway Atlas 1970 Ian Allan

British Railway Companies by Christopher Awdry *Patrick Stephens Limited*

British Railways Past and Present No 3 The North West by Paul Shannon & John Hillmer *Past & Present Publishing.*

British Railways Past and Present No 39 Liverpool and Wirral by Paul Shannon & John Hillmer *Past & Present Publishing*

British Railways Past and Present No 40 Cheshire by Paul Shannon & John Hillmer *Past & Present Publishing*

British Railways Past and Present No 43 West, East and North Lancashire by Paul Shannon & John Hillmer *Past & Present Publishing*

Complete British Railways Maps and Gazetteer from 1830 to 1981 by C. J. Wignall *OPC*

Liverpool Road Station, Manchester An historical and architectural survey by R. S. Fitzgerald *Manchester University Press.*

Liverpool to Manchester into the second century by N. Fiels, A. C. Gilbert and N. R. Knight *Manchester Transport Museum Society*

Lost Lines Liverpool and Mersey by Nigel Welbourn *Ian Allan*

Lost Railways of Cheshire by Leslie Oppitz *Countryside Books*

Introduction

People have always had a fascination with disused railway lines and stations. Ever since the opening of the first railway lines in the 1820s, stations have been closing, many in the last century because they were resited to more suitable locations. This is particularly true in London, where many of the London termini were originally built some distance short of their present site.

In the early 20th century, stations and lines began to close with the introduction of new bus services, the increased popularity of the car and improvements in roads. Other lines and stations never lived up to the expectations of their promoters.

Many rural stations were badly sited, well away from the towns and villages they were designed to serve, and this too led to a rapid decline in passenger numbers when more convenient forms of transport became available.

The steady trickle of railway closures increased in the 1950s, turning into a torrent in the 1960s with the rationalisation of our railway network under the infamous Dr Richard Beeching, Chairman of British Railways from 1961 to 1965.

In March 1963 his report, *The Reshaping of British Railways*, was published. The 'Beeching Axe', as it became known, proposed a massive closure programme. He recommended the closure of one-third of Britain's 18,000-mile railway network, mainly rural branches and cross-country lines, and 2,128 stations on lines that were to be kept open. The following year his second report, *The Development of the Major Railway Trunk Routes*, was even more scathing, with a proposal that all lines should be closed apart from the major intercity routes and important profit-making commuter lines around the big cities, leaving Britain with little more than a skeleton railway system and large parts of the country entirely devoid of railways. The report was rejected by the Government and Dr Beeching resigned in 1965.

Although Beeching was gone, the closure programme that he started under the Conservatives in the early 1960s continued unabated under Labour until it was brought to a halt in the early 1970s, but by that time the damage had been done. In 1955 the British railway system consisted of 20,000 miles of track and 6,000 stations. By 1975 this had shrunk to 12,000 miles of track and 2,000 stations, roughly the same size as it is today.

Lost Railways of Lancashire by Gordon Suggitt *Countryside Books*

Lost Railways of Merseyside and Greater Manchester by Gordon Suggitt *Countryside Books*

Merseyrail Electrics The Inside Story by T. B. Maud *NBC books*

Paddington to the Mersey, The GWR's forgotten route from London to Birkenhead by Dr R. Preston Hendry & R. Powell Hendry *OPC*

Rail Centres Manchester by Stanley Hall *Ian Allan*

Rails to Port and Starboard by John W. Gahan *Countyvise Limited*

Railway Passenger Stations in Great Britain by Michael Quick *RCHS*

Railway Stations of Merseyside and District by Paul Bolger *The Bluecoat Press*

Seaport to Seaside Lines to Southport and Ormskirk 13 Decades of trains and Travel by John W. Gahan *Countyvise Limited*

Seventeen Stations to Dingle The Liverpool Overhead Railway Remembered by John W. Gahan *Countyvise Limited*

The Dockers Umbrella by Paul Bolger *The Bluecoat Press*

The Lancashire & Yorkshire Railway Volume 2 by John Marshall *David and Charles*

The Midland Route From Manchester Part One Central to New Mills via Didsbury, Stockport & Marple by E. M. Johnson *Foxline Publishing*

The Oxford Companion to British Railway History by Jack Simmons & Gordon Biddle *Oxford*

The St Helens Railway its Rivals and Successors by J. M. Tolston *Oakwood Press*

Back Issues of

British Railways Illustrated, Backtrack, Railway World, Steam Days, The Railway Magazine

And extensive use of Ordnance Survey sheet maps both past and present

Gradually the memory of these lost lines and stations began to fade as the urban sites were redeveloped with perhaps only a road name to remind people of their former existence. Most of the rural sites were returned to nature and agriculture, although many of the stations still survive in some form or another, some transformed into attractive country dwellings while others linger on in the undergrowth, abandoned and forgotten.

In 2005 Nick Catford, a member of Subterranea Britannica, started the 'Disused Stations' website with the aim of creating a definitive database of the UK's closed stations that would be freely available to all. The work to complete the database is still ongoing and will take many years to complete. To date there are 1,413 stations on the site and it is visited by thousands of people every week.

This book is intended to act as a companion to the 'Disused Stations' website. It follows roughly the same format but, as a book, it should appeal to those who want to have something tangible to put on their bookshelf, and also to those who want to go out and visit the sites of the stations, as it can be used as a guide book.

With so many stations now on the website it was difficult to decide which should be included in this book. The idea of selecting terminus stations from the North West, an area steeped in railway history, seemed like a good starting point. In this book they appear in chronological order of opening, as it was felt that this would be a good way of showing how the network developed, expanded and eventually contracted.

Paul Wright

Key to headings:

STATION NAME	Indicates station closed to passengers pre-nationalisation
STATION NAME	Indicates station closed to passengers post-nationalisation

Above **Liverpool Crown Street:** A view looking east at the entrance to Crown Street Station as seen in May 1972. The building seen in the picture dates from the first half of the 19th century and may well have been present when the station opened in 1830. It is not however part of the passenger station which was demolished shortly after closure. In all likelihood it was provided as an office facility for the goods depot. It had clearly been altered during its existance and was last used by a scrap metal merchant. *The Bob Webb Collection*

Left **Liverpool Crown Street:** Looking north-east at the site of the station in October 2005. *Paul Wright*

Right **Liverpool Crown Street:** The site of the station and coal yard looking north-west in October 2005, showing the Wapping Tunnel ventilation shaft. *Paul Wright*

LIVERPOOL Crown Street (1830)

Date opened:	15 September 1830
Location:	East side of Crown Street near its junction with Myrtle Street
Company on opening:	Liverpool & Manchester Railway
Date closed to passengers:	15 August 1836
Date closed completely:	1 May 1972
Company on closing:	Liverpool & Manchester Railway
Present state:	Demolished – site is now a public park
County:	Lancashire (modern county of Merseyside)
OS Grid Ref:	SJ364897

Crown Street was the original western passenger terminus of the Liverpool & Manchester Railway, the world's first railway to cater for passengers as one of its primary functions. It was also arguably the world's first intercity railway.

Crown Street was situated at the end of a single-track tunnel that led up to the station from Edge Hill. Locomotives only went as far as Edge Hill to an engine

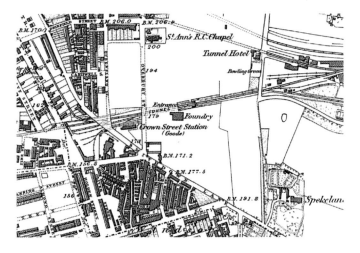

transfer point, the site of the famous Moorish Arch and also the point at which the Wapping Tunnel, which led down to the docks, started. Coaches were cable-worked *up* to Crown Street and proceeded by gravity from the station down to Edge Hill.

The station was provided with a two-storey sandstone building in typical Georgian style. A simple low-level platform was provided for departing trains. Three lines passed through the station, which was provided with an overall roof to give passengers protection from the elements.

Such was the monumental success of the Liverpool & Manchester Railway that Crown Street passenger terminus soon proved inadequate due to its size and distance from the city centre, and it was closed on 15 August 1836. A new terminus was opened at Lime Street, much closer to the city centre. It is not known when the station building was demolished but it is likely that it did not survive long after closure. There are no known photographs of the original station building, only a painting dating from 1831 by Thomas Berry.

The station site, which was connected to Edge Hill by a further tunnel in the 1840s, became a goods depot, and remained open as a rail-served coal depot until as recently as 1972. Today the site is a landscaped public park, and no sign of the original tunnel that linked the station to Edge Hill, which was built in 1829, remains – it is still there, but buried at its western portal.

The later 1840s tunnel can still be seen at the top end of the site close to the children's play area. It is still rail-served and is used as a head shunt for freight trains that arrive at Edge Hill.

Right **Liverpool Crown Street:** The later 1840s Crown Street Tunnel, seen in October 2005. *Paul Wright*

Below **Liverpool Crown Street:** At Edge Hill the new Crown Street Tunnel is on the left, Wapping Tunnel in the centre and the original Crown Street Tunnel, leading to Crown Street station, on the right. *Paul Wright*

MANCHESTER Liverpool Road (1830)

Date opened:	15 September 1830
Location:	On north side of Liverpool Road in Manchester's Castlefields district
Company on opening:	Liverpool & Manchester Railway
Date closed to passengers:	4 May 1844
Date closed completely:	1975
Company on closing:	London & North Western Railway
Present state:	Largely intact, as part of the Manchester Museum of Science and Industry
County:	Lancashire (modern county of Greater Manchester)
OS Grid Ref:	SJ829979

Manchester Liverpool Road was the eastern passenger terminus of George Stephenson's Liverpool & Manchester Railway, which opened for business on 15 September 1830. The line was the world's first to be constructed with the carriage of passengers as one of its main activities. It was also arguably the world's first true intercity railway.

As the line was the first of its kind a great deal of thought was devoted to how to create passenger facilities. The only transport hubs that existed at the time where the points from which road coaches departed. These tended to be large inns, which could cater for passengers who might need to stay overnight and which had stabling facilities for horses. However, coaching inns did not really offer a good model for a railway terminus. The other issue facing the line's builders was where to locate the terminus in Manchester. The original plans for the railway would have seen a station developed on the west side of the

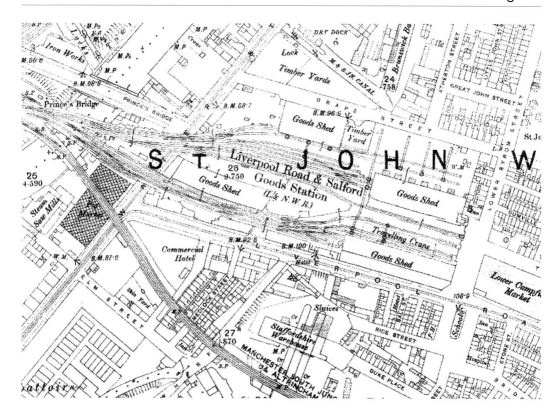

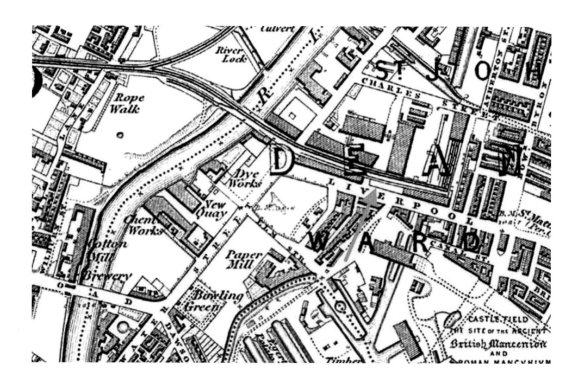

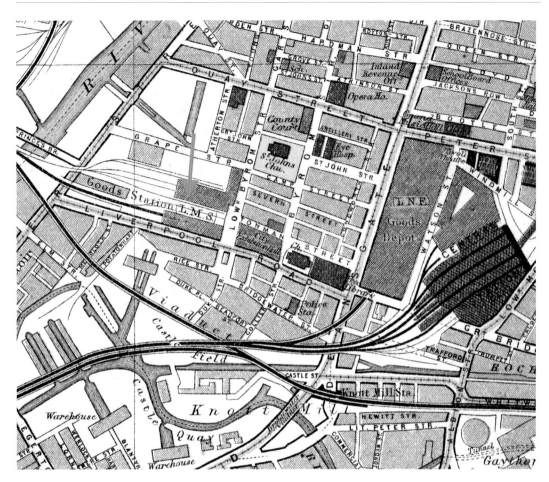

Left **Manchester Liverpool Road:** The station is seen during the 150th anniversary celebrations of the Liverpool & Manchester Railway in 1980. *Bevan Price*

River Irwell in the town of Salford. However, the line's promoters wanted to have a terminus in Manchester proper, which would save passengers from having to cross the river. A site was therefore identified and purchased at Liverpool Road on the western edge of the city.

To reach the site the line had to be raised to an elevation exceeding 29 feet so that a bridge could be built across the Irwell that would still allow navigation by the boats of the Irwell Navigation Company. A fine sandstone bridge consisting of two arches was built over the river; this was connected to a viaduct, which was followed by another bridge that crossed the busy thoroughfare of Water Street. This last bridge carried the line to the site that had been chosen for the station.

An existing house was purchased on Liverpool Road and a handsome two-storey stone building was constructed next to it to cater for passengers. The house was used as the station superintendent's office. The

railway was at the level of the first storey of the building, and was reached by staircases leading up to a simple platform with a covered canopy to shelter passengers from the rain. Interestingly, this platform was to be used only by departing trains. For passengers arriving at Liverpool Road a simple platform was provided on the western side of the Water Street bridge. At first no facilities where provided there, as it was assumed that arriving passengers would quickly disperse into Manchester. However, this situation changed in 1837 when an arrival station was built.

Passengers departing from Manchester were separated by class, with the more affluent citizens enjoying the better facilities.

The passenger facilities were small in comparison to the goods facilities provided at the station. A fine brick-built warehouse was provided opposite the departure platform, then within seven years four more warehouses where added, demonstrating the phenomenal success of the line.

Below **Manchester Liverpool Road:**
The Irwell Bridge, which carried the line into the station, seen from the east bank of the river in July 2006. *Paul Wright*

By 1844 the station was far too small to cope with the passenger numbers using the line, for trains were now travelling to more destinations than just Liverpool. A new station was therefore opened further to the east, known as Victoria, and Liverpool Road closed to passengers.

The station site continued to be developed as a goods facility and in 1905 the original Water Street bridge was demolished to allow widening of the street; surprisingly, however, the former passenger station survived mainly intact, including the original 1st Class staircase.

Above **Manchester Liverpool Road:** The station frontage on Liverpool Road in July 2006. The house at the corner of Liverpool Road and Water Street predated the station, and was bought by the L&MR and used as the superintendent's office and living quarters. *Paul Wright*

Left **Manchester Liverpool Road:** The station frontage in July 2006, showing the 1st Class entrance. *Paul Wright*

Left **Manchester Liverpool Road:** The station site looking west towards Liverpool in July 2006. The departure platform is on the left, while to the right can be seen the original 1830 warehouse. *Paul Wright*

Below **Manchester Liverpool Road:** A bracket that once held a bell. In the early years the bell was rung when trains were due to depart. Later the bell was replaced with a clock. *Paul Wright*

In 1975 the station closed completely, but in 1980 the site was used to celebrate the 150th anniversary of the Liverpool & Manchester Railway. Locomotives visited from all over the country and the local authority had the idea of creating a Science and Industry Museum that would preserve and make good use of the site. Today that Museum is a reality, and visitors can view the station site and see the 1st Class booking hall restored to its 1830 condition. A replica locomotive of the era, *Planet*, can regularly be seen in steam at the station site.

Left **Manchester Liverpool Road:** The 1st Class booking hall has been restored to its 1830 condition and is now part of the Museum of Science and Industry. *Paul Wright*

Below **Manchester Liverpool Road:** A replica of L&MR loco *Planet* at Manchester Liverpool Road station in July 2006 *Paul Wright*

WARRINGTON Dallam Lane (1831)

Date opened:	25 July 1831
Location:	North of Tannery Lane and west of Dallam Lane
Company on opening:	Warrington & Newton Railway
Date closed to passengers:	4 July 1837
Date closed completely:	1960s
Company on closing:	Grand Junction Railway
Present state:	Demolished – site is now occupied by a community centre
County:	Lancashire (modern county of Cheshire)
OS Grid Ref:	SJ606888

Warrington Dallam Lane station opened as the southern terminus of the Warrington & Newton Railway's line linking the town of Warrington with the Liverpool & Manchester Railway at Earlestown. The branch thus allowed passengers and goods to be conveyed between Warrington and the important cities of Liverpool and Manchester.

Dallam Lane station opened with the line on 25 July 1831. Stations at this time were usually fairly basic affairs, and in all likelihood the station would have consisted of a simple track-level arrival and departure platform. A three-storey brick building provided booking facilities, and passenger services operated to points along the Liverpool & Manchester line.

On 4 July 1837 the Grand Junction Railway opened from Birmingham to a point north of Dallam Lane station, allowing trains to travel between Birmingham and Liverpool and Manchester, but bypassing Dallam Lane, which was replaced by another station on the new main line. The original station closed on 4 July 1837 with the opening of the new facility.

The Dallam Lane site continued in use as a rail-served goods station right up until the 1960s.

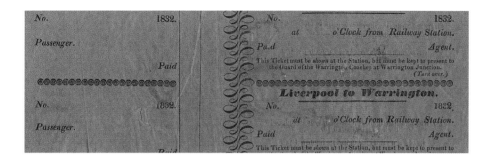

Below **Warrington Dallam Lane:** A view looking south towards the site of the station taken during a visit by a rail tour in 1967. The line leading off towards the left of the picture would have led into the station. By this date the location was an extensive goods station. *Bevan Price*

Left **Warrington Dallam Lane**: A view of the station site looking north in October 2008. The line ran between the gaps in the buildings and shared its course with the lane itself. *Paul Wright*

Right **Warrington Dallam Lane:** A view of the Three Pigeons public house – the station was situated behind it, the line passing to its right. A pub of that name stood here during the time that the station was open and provided a ticket sales office and waiting facilities. *Paul Wright*

Right **Warrington Dallam Lane:** A view looking south at the site of the station in October 2008. *Paul Wright*

Left **Warrington Dallam Lane:** A view looking north away from the site of the station in 1967, showing the goods station that was then still in use. *Bevan Price*

RUNCORN GAP (First 1833)

Date opened:	September 1833
Location:	Just north of St Helens Canal within Spike Island park
Company on opening:	St Helens & Runcorn Gap Railway
Date closed to passengers:	1 July 1852
Date closed completely:	1 July 1852
Company on closing:	St Helens Canal & Railway Company
Present state:	Demolished
County:	Lancashire (modern county of Cheshire)
OS Grid Ref:	SJ516847

Runcorn Gap station was the southern terminus of the St Helens & Runcorn Gap Railway, which ran from St Helens in the north to the banks of the Mersey at Widnes in the south, with no intermediate stations. The line was one of the earliest railways and was under construction before George Stephenson had completed the famous Liverpool & Manchester

Runcorn Gap: A brake-van tour takes on water at Widnes Dock Junction in August 1967. The train is standing at a point just to the north of the site of Runcorn Gap station. *Bevan Price*

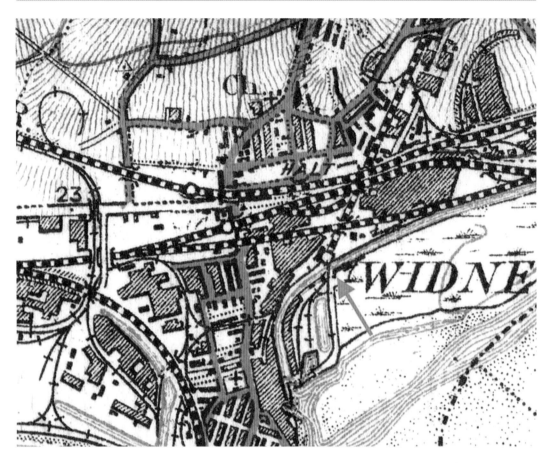

Railway, which the Runcorn Gap line crossed to the south of St Helens.

The line opened on 21 February 1833, but very little thought had been given to the provision of passenger services. The primary purpose had been to move coal to the Mersey for transhipment to barges that would then go down river to Liverpool. A dock, named Widnes Dock, with extensive facilities, including rail connections, was laid out at Runcorn Gap; it is believed that this was the world's first direct rail-to-ship facility of this kind.

The people of St Helens lobbied the St Helens & Runcorn Gap Railway Company for a passenger service to Runcorn Gap. As a result, in September 1833 the company hired two coaches from the L&MR at £1 per coach per week and began a service. No specific passenger trains were run – the coaches were attached to coal trains. It was at this time that Runcorn Gap station opened. No pictures of it exist, but early maps show the most basic

of facilities. In all likelihood it would have been nothing more than a simple cottage-type structure. It was situated on the north side of the St Helens Canal, which opened its extension to Runcorn Gap on 24 July 1833. The railway crossed the canal to the south of the station by means of a swing bridge.

In 1838 more than 26,000 passengers used the line, but very little thought was given to them. The line did not even submit a timetable for Bradshaw's *Railway Guide*, which began in 1839. Passengers made numerous complaints about it; it had two steep inclines on its route,

Opposite **Runcorn Gap:** Seen during the same tour in August 1967, the line in the foreground is the east-to-south spur connection from the Garston line to the Warrington line. The next two tracks are the Widnes to St Helens main line, the original St Helens & Runcorn Gap Railway, and behind them are factory sidings on which the locomotive is standing as it takes on water. The site of Runcorn Gap station is just out of view to the left. *Bevan Price*

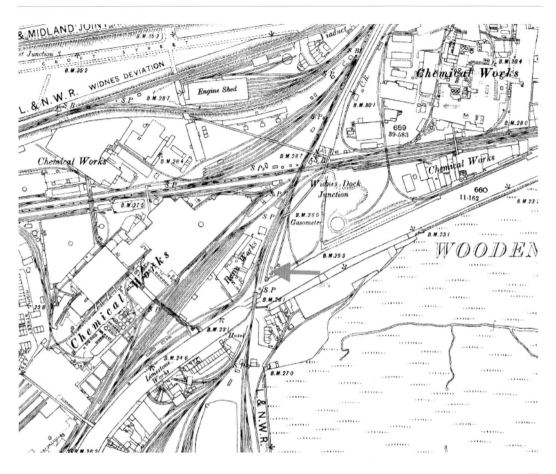

one just north of Runcorn Gap, and trains were hauled up them by cable. There is a record of a passenger who arrived at Runcorn Gap station in the early 1840s to find the train gone. The Station Master sold him a ticket and said, 'If you rush along the line you will easily catch it up.' Such was the quality of the service.

From 1845 the line was doubled and the inclines eased, which gave a journey time of only 25 minutes from St Helens to Runcorn Gap, but still passenger facilities and services did not much improve.

On 1 July 1852 the St Helens & Runcorn Gap company, by then known as St Helens Canal & Railway Company, opened its line to Garston, and on this occasion more consideration was given to passengers. A new station was opened, also called Runcorn Gap

Above **Runcorn Gap:** The site of the station in December 2005, looking north from the south side of the St Helens Canal. The station was located just to the north of the swing bridge, the footings for which can clearly be seen in the picture. *Paul Wright*

but much closer to Widnes town centre, so more convenient. Upon the opening of the new station the original Runcorn Gap station closed.

The line through the site of the station continued in use for goods services until November 1968, after which the tracks where lifted. The swing bridge that carried the line across the St Helens Canal to Widnes Dock survived until the early 1980s, when the whole area was laid out as a park and it was replaced by a wooden footbridge.

ST HELENS (first, 1833)

Date opened:	September 1833
Location:	About 100 yards east of Linkway East (A58)
Company on opening:	St Helens & Runcorn Gap Railway Companyy
Date closed to passengers:	18 December 1849
Date closed completely:	18 December 1849
Company on closing:	St Helens Canal & Railway Company
Present state:	No trace remains – exact location is difficult to pinpoint
County:	Lancashire (modern county of Merseyside)
OS Grid Ref:	SJ517949 (approximate)

St Helens's first station was the northern terminus of the St Helens & Runcorn Gap Railway, which ran from St Helens in the north to the banks of the Mersey at Widnes in the south, with no intermediate stations. It crossed the Liverpool & Manchester Railway south of St Helens (see the Runcorn Gap section above).

The first train, consisting of coal wagons, passed along the entire route on 28 February 1832, then in September 1833 the company began a passenger service between St Helens and the junction station on the L&MR, and also to Runcorn Gap, where the coaches were attached to coal trains. Interestingly, some services down to the junction were horse-drawn, and they were certainly in use in 1835, as Sir George Head, in his book *A Home Tour Through the Manufacturing Districts of England in the Summer of 1835*, explained how 'we all got into one large covered vehicle, and were dragged at a foot pace, by a single horse, along the branch railroad, about a mile in length, that leads to the

Above **St Helens (first station):** Looking east along the Ravenhead branch in November 1990 – the station site was probably at the extreme left of this photograph. *Bevan Price*

town. It must be confessed that the present mode of conveyance was as disagreeable and slow as can well be imagined.' Services down to the L&MR were advertised by that company, and St Helens's first station dates from this period.

The station was located a short distance to the west of the former Ravenhead Junction, and was not ideally situated for the town. It was a very basic affair and was replaced in 1849 by a second station at Raven Street in the town centre.

Over the intervening years the area was much altered, but it remained a railway location until the early 1990s. It has been very much changed since the opening of the St Helens Linkway road system, which occupies part of the alignment of the Ravenhead branch.

Above **St Helens (first station):** Looking east towards Ravenhead Junction in November 1990. The station site is thought to have been somewhere beyond the bridge. *Bevan Price*

Left **St Helens (first station):** This picture was taken from an approximately similar angle to that above, but from a greater distance (from the Linkway East embankment) in February 2006. The station site is thought to be in the wooded area behind the brickwork. *Bevan Price*

BIRKENHEAD Monks Ferry (1844)

Date opened:	23 October 1844
Location:	East of the Ivy Street, Monks Ferry, Church Street road junction
Company on opening:	Chester & Birkenhead Railway
Date closed to passengers:	31 March 1878
Date closed completely:	Mid-1960s
Company on closing:	GWR and LNWR
Present state:	Demolished
County:	Cheshire (modern county of Merseyside)
OS Grid Ref:	SJ329887

The first railway to reach Birkenhead was the Chester & Birkenhead Railway, which opened a temporary terminus at Grange Lane on 23 September 1840. Four years later the line was extended to a new terminus on the banks of the Mersey, known as Monks Ferry, which opened on 23 October 1844. The station was located at the end of a single-track tunnel that ran to the site of Grange Lane, where a new station, Birkenhead Town, was provided.

The station became an important northern outpost for the Great Western Railway, which operated express services to London Paddington. Monks Ferry gave the GWR a foothold in Liverpool, which was connected to the station by means of a steam ferry across the Mersey. The station was provided with two platforms, giving three platform faces, two of which were covered by an overall roof to afford protection from the elements, which at this riverside location was not an unimportant consideration.

Eventually the station became too small for the growing passenger traffic, and on 31 March 1878 the Great Western Railway and the London & North Western Railway opened a new terminus at Birkenhead Woodside. This led to the closure of Monks Ferry, which was used thereafter for many years as a goods depot.

Today the site is occupied by apartment blocks and the only evidence of the station ever having existed is a sandstone wall that formed part of an overbridge at the west end of the station.

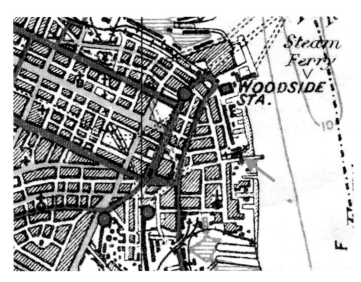

Opposite top **Birkenhead Monks Ferry:** The remains of the station in August 1965. *Robin Lush*

Opposite bottom **Birkenhead Monks Ferry:** The Monks Ferry Landing Stage. *Paul Wright*

Right **Birkenhead Monks Ferry:** The site of the station, looking west. *Paul Wright*

Right **Birkenhead Monks Ferry:** The station site looking east, showing how the station was located on the banks of the River Mersey. At one time a ferry crossed to Liverpool from here. *Paul Wright*

Below **Birkenhead Monks Ferry:** The only evidence of the station is the bridge wall on Church Street. The line ran under the street, then in a deep cutting for a short distance before entering a tunnel to Birkenhead Town. This view is looking towards the Town station. *Paul Wright*

ST HELENS (second, 1849)

Date opened:	19 December 1849
Location:	South side of Church Street on what is now Chalon Way
Company on opening:	St Helens Canal & Railway Company
Date closed to passengers:	1 February 1858
Date closed completely:	By 1871
Company on closing:	St Helens Canal & Railway Company
Present state:	No trace remains – site occupied by roads
County:	Lancashire (modern county of Merseyside)
OS Grid Ref:	SJ515953

St Helens's second station replaced the previous St Helens & Runcorn Gap Railway's northern terminus, which was situated some distance from the town.

The new station was located conveniently close to the town centre opposite the town's Raven Inn, which still stands today. Contemporary maps show 13 lines, sidings and bays at the

Above **St Helens (second station):** Looking north-west towards the site of the station in February 2006. *Bevan Price*

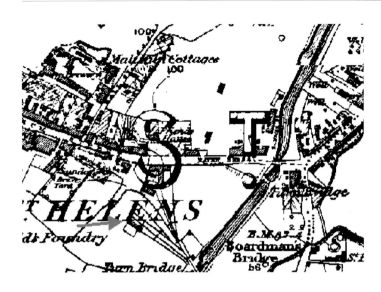

Below **St Helens (second station):** Looking north towards the site of the station in February 2006 *Bevan Price*

station site, which gives the impression of a significant location. However, a local historian writing some 40 years after its opening described it as a 'small, rudely constructed erection'.

The station was destined to have only a very short life, due to the building of a new line by the St Helens Canal & Railway from St Helens to Rainford. The way that this line connected with the original line meant that passenger trains would have had to reverse at the terminus to reach Rainford; this would have

been unsatisfactory, so it was decided to build a new St Helens station (the third) on what became the through line.

The second station duly closed with the opening of the new facilities on 1 February 1858, but remained in use as a goods depot until well into the second half of the 20th century. Remarkably, in 1959, during demolition of one of the station buildings, thought to have been the booking office, passenger receipts from the period were found.

LIVERPOOL Exchange (1850)

Date opened:	13 May 1850
Location:	Tithebarn Street
Company on opening:	Lancashire & Yorkshire Railway and East Lancashire Railway
Date closed to passengers:	20 April 1977
Date closed completely:	20 April 1977
Company on closing:	British Rail (London Midland Region)
Present state:	Station frontage, at one time a hotel, has been converted into the Mercury Court office complex. Trainshed was demolished shortly after closure and the site is now a car park. Elements of the former station can still be seen throughout the car park site.
County:	Lancashire (modern county of Merseyside)
OS Grid Ref:	SJ343908

In the 1840s two lines where constructed into Liverpool from the north. The first was from Bury via Bolton and Wigan, and would ultimately have connections to Manchester, providing an alternative route to that offered by the Liverpool & Manchester Railway of 1830. The Bury line was ultimately constructed by the Lancashire & Yorkshire Railway. The second line came in from Preston and was constructed by the East Lancashire Railway. The lines met at Walton, then shared a route into Liverpool. On 20 November 1848 the companies opened a joint terminus at Great Howard Street; however, they made uneasy bedfellows and could not even agree on a joint name for the station. The LYR favoured Borough Goal, after the nearby prison, while the ELR favoured Great Howard Street.

In the event this station soon proved inadequate for the heavy traffic that developed, and an extension was soon under way to a point right on the edge of the city business district at Tithebarn Street. This new station opened on 13 May 1850 and was known by two names: to the LYR it was Exchange, and to the ELR it was Tithebarn Street. The new station was a grand affair that had required the demolition of 540 houses in an area that had become a notorious slum. It was 25 feet above street level, being supported on brick arches. The station frontage was a two-storey affair in the 'Italianate' style, and was connected to Tithebarn Street by a set of steps. It had five platforms, which were provided with an overall roof for the comfort of passengers.

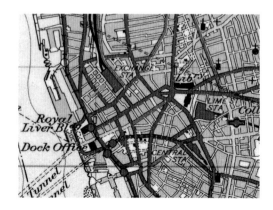

One platform was used for arrivals and two platforms were allocated to each of the railway companies for departures. Each company also had its own offices, booking facilities and waiting rooms. With the opening of the station

the original terminus at Great Howard Street was developed as a major goods station.

On 1 October 1850 a line from Southport was connected to the ELR and LYR line north of Sandhills, which allowed trains from the seaside town to access the new station, providing even more traffic. Although a minor line, it grew very quickly as a commuter route, with housing development spreading all along it.

On 13 August 1859 the ELR was absorbed into the LYR and the station became known by the latter's name

Above **Liverpool Exchange:** This was the station on 4 June 1967. *Bevan Price*

Left **Liverpool Exchange:** The station on 8 July 1967. *Bevan Price*

Left **Liverpool Exchange:** The approach to Exchange in 1963, seen from the station signal box. *Phil Williams*

Below **Liverpool Exchange:** An electric baggage car at Exchange in 1956. *Dewi Williams*

of Liverpool Exchange. By the 1870s traffic had built up to such a degree that further expansion was needed. Widening of the station was sanctioned in 1876, but nothing was done and the situation went from bad to worse. Finally an Act of 24 July 1882 authorised a widening of the approach lines, whilst an Act of 2 August 1883 allowed for a complete rebuild of Exchange.

The new station opened in part on 12 December 1886 and completely on 2 July 1888. In this its final form, Exchange consisted of a grand hotel frontage behind which was located a covered cab road. Further buildings

Above **Liverpool Exchange:** The station seen from Liverpool Exchange No 2 signal box in 1973. By this time decline had set in and the station had lost its Anglo-Scottish services. At this date, however, platforms 4 to 10 were still in use. Electric services ran to both Southport and Ormskirk, while DMU services operated to Wigan, Bolton and Manchester Victoria. *Tony Graham*

Left **Liverpool Exchange:** The station frontage in January 2005. *Paul Wright*

provided office space, booking and waiting facilities. The station had 10 platform faces protected from the elements by four longitudinal gabled roofs. By this time the station was served by long-distance trains running north to Blackpool, the Lake District and Scotland, and east to the cotton towns of Lancashire and onwards to Yorkshire. An express service to Manchester competed directly with that of the Cheshire Lines Committee, which ran out of Liverpool Central, and the LNWR, which ran out of Liverpool Lime Street. Exchange also catered for an extensive network of commuter services.

On 22 March 1904 the LYR electrified its Southport Line. This was one of the first main lines to be electrified in Britain and proved a great success, generating even more commuter business. Following this success, electrification was extended along the Preston line as far as Aintree on 3 December 1906. Over the next few years it would be extended twice more until it reached Ormskirk on 1 April 1913. Commuter services out of Exchange became even more intense after electrification, and long-distance services became faster. When the LYR became part of the LMS in 1923 regular Manchester expresses completed the journey in 40 minutes.

Being located fairly close to the Docks, Liverpool Exchange was extensively damaged during the Second World War, causing major disruption to services and the loss of part of the station roof, which was not replaced. At one point during 1941 the station was out of use for three months.

After the war the station remained as busy as ever, and even after nationalisation in 1948 very little changed at first. In 1960 destinations from Exchange included Preston, Ormskirk, Rochdale, Blackpool Central, Aintree Sefton Arms, Southport, Manchester Victoria, Bradford Exchange, Leeds Central, Glasgow Central, Edinburgh Princes Street, Newcastle and Windermere. However, by the end of the decade many of the express services had been diverted to the nearby Lime Street station. One service that did remain was the Liverpool to Glasgow Sunday express, which during the summer of 1968 became the last scheduled BR passenger service to use steam power, steam haulage continuing until August of that year.

By 1970 the last express service, the Liverpool Exchange to Glasgow Central, had been diverted to Lime Street, leaving only the busy electric commuter services to Ormskirk and Southport and a DMU service to Wigan, Bolton and Manchester. The station took on an air of dereliction, not helped by the removal of the lines from platforms 1 to 3 after the loss of main-line services. By the mid-1970s only platforms 4 to 7 remained in use.

For decades there had been proposals to link Liverpool's three termini (Exchange, Central High Level and Lime Street) with an extension to the underground Mersey Railway. Work on the construction of an underground loop and link line finally began in the early 1970s. A new underground station was built at Moorfields, only metres away from the entrance to Liverpool Exchange, and a new alignment was built to take the approach lines

Above **Liverpool Exchange:** Part of the side wall still in place along Pall Mall in January 2005. *Paul Wright*

Left **Liverpool Exchange:** No 2 signal box in 1977, showing the approach lines coming into the station from the north. By this date the track layout had been severely rationalised, as the station was to close at the end of April. *Tony Graham*

to Exchange down to this station. Electrification would also be extended along the former Bury line to Kirkby.

On 20 April 1977 Liverpool Exchange station closed, and several days later trains were diverted to the new underground link line. The last train to leave was an enthusiasts' special put on to mark the closure of the station. Its destination was Liverpool Lime Street, less than a mile away. However, to get there it had to travel via Wigan and St Helens, a round trip of more than 40 miles.

Above **Liverpool Exchange:** Surviving remains of the station in January 2005. *Paul Wright*

Below left **Liverpool Exchange:** The station frontage in May 1981. *Nick Catford*

Below **Liverpool Exchange:** The John Pearson memorial. *Paul Wright*

The new link line now forms part of the Merseyrail Northern Line linking Hunts Cross in the south of the city with the northern destinations of Southport, Ormskirk and Kirkby.

Above **Liverpool Exchange:** A view towards the buffer stops at Liverpool Exchange on 11 April 1977, showing a DMU and former LMS third rail EMUs, built to serve the Southport and Ormskirk lines. *Robin Lush*

Below **Liverpool Exchange:** Between the station hotel building and the train shed was a taxi circulating area. It is seen here on 11 April 1977, only a few weeks before the station's closure. *Robin Lush*

Liverpool Exchange: Two views looking towards the buffer stops, showing the station to be in poor condition on 11 April 1977 – most of the glass from the roof is missing. The station would close a few weeks later. *Both Robin Lush*

BACUP (1852)

Date opened:	1 October 1852
Location:	Rockcliffe Road
Company on opening:	East Lancashire Railway
Date closed to passengers:	5 December 1966
Date closed completely:	1968
Company on closing:	British Rail (London Midland Region)
Present state:	Demolished – the site has been developed with industrial units
County:	Lancashire (modern county of Greater Manchester)
OS Grid Ref:	SD868224

Bacup station opened as a terminus in the town on 1 February 1853, at the end of a line that ran from Manchester through Bury and Rawtenstall. The line had opened in stages, the Manchester to Rawtenstall section opening to passengers on 28 September 1846. The next section, from Rawtenstall to Waterfoot, opened to passengers on 27 March 1848. However, between Waterfoot and Bacup there was a formidable natural obstacle called the 'Thrutch Gorge', better known today as 'The Glenn'. Tunnelling was required at this location, and it was another four years before passenger trains began running from Waterfoot to Bacup, on 1 October 1852. Initially this section was single track, but it was doubled in 1880, which of course meant the need to excavate another tunnel.

On 1 December 1881 a line was opened from Rochdale to Bacup, and the station was rebuilt. It consisted of a wide single island platform that provided two platform faces. A single-storey brick building was located at the north end of the station, facing onto the street. A substantial platform awning

Right **Bacup:** A view of the station in the early part of the 20th century, probably taken from the top of a factory chimney. *Wendy Lord collection*

was provided, which gave passengers protection from the weather. Goods sidings and a cattle dock were also provided.

Initially most passenger services ran to Manchester via Clifton, then, after 1879, via Prestwich. After 1916 services were diverted to run south of Bury via Heywood. This was because the line from Manchester Victoria to Bury had been electrified, and passengers from Bacup and other stations on the line tended to change at Bury to the electric service. After a

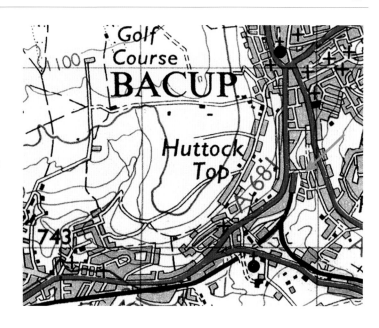

Below **Bacup:** A view of the station after closure, looking north. *Wendy Lord collection*

Above **Bacup:** A view looking south along the platform in the early 1960s. *Wendy Lord collection*

Below **Bacup:** The grey shed on the eft of the picture stands on the site of Bacup station. When the station was open there was a single-storey roadside building, located next to the cottages. *Paul Wright*

few years most Bacup line services terminated at Bury. From 1881 services also ran to Rochdale, but they were never as frequent as services on the Manchester line. Indeed, they were subject to very early competition from the Rochdale Electric Tramway, which opened in 1911. Passenger traffic to Rochdale from Bacup ended on 16 June 1947.

Travel from Bacup to Bury took approximately 32 to 34 minutes, and a minute or two longer was added for journeys from Bury to Bacup to compensate for the gradients. Trains made a shorter trip to Ramsbottom every evening, returning

Above **Bacup:** In this view, looking north in October 2008, the ramp that led down to the goods sidings can clearly be seen. *Paul Wright*

Below **Bacup:** A view of the station site looking north in October 2008, now occupied by the large industrial shed that dominates the view. *Paul Wright*

at 6.37pm. There was also a through train from Bolton to Bacup each day, leaving Bolton at 9.00am and due into Bacup at 9.48am, travelling via Radcliffe, but with no corresponding service in the reverse direction.

Diesel multiple units (DMUs) were introduced in 1956, when there was a train every 30 minutes each way, leaving Bury at 20 past and 10 to the hour, and returning from Bacup on the hour and half-hour. Journey time was reduced to 28 minutes from Bacup to Bury, but was 34 minutes in the reverse direction.

Despite this extensive service the section of line from Rawtenstall to Bacup was selected for closure, which took place on 5 December 1966. It continued in use for goods for a short time, but was lifted in October 1968. Passenger services continued to run as far as Bury until 3 June 1972.

Bacup station was demolished after closure and today the site is occupied by industrial units.

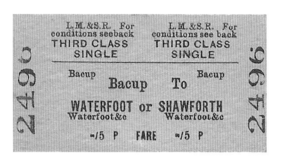

Bacup: A view looking at the buffer stops at Bacup station during a visit by a rail tour in 1962. *Bevan Price*

GARSTON DOCK (1852)

Date opened:	1 July 1852
Location:	East of junction of Dock Road and Garston Way
Company on opening:	St Helens Canal & Railway Company
Date closed to passengers:	16 June 1947
Date closed completely:	16 June 1947
Company on closing:	London Midland & Scottish Railway
Present state:	Demolished – site is now occupied by a bypass
County:	Lancashire (modern county of Merseyside)
OS Grid Ref:	SJ400847

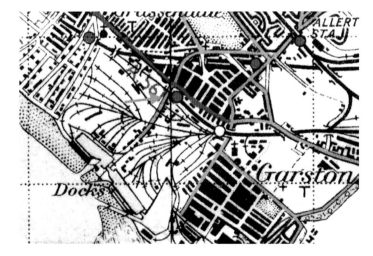

Garston Dock station started life as the western terminus of the St Helens Canal & Railway Company's line from Widnes to Garston, which opened on 1 July 1852, and finished life as the southern terminus of the Liverpool Lime Street to Garston Dock line of the LMS.

When the line first opened, passengers were carried forward to Liverpool by horse-drawn omnibuses, a state of affairs that could never compete with the LNWR's Liverpool to Manchester line. To address this, on 1 June 1864 an extension was opened by the Garston & Liverpool Railway, which ran to a terminus closer to the city at Brunswick. On 5 July this extension became part of the CLC. On 15 February 1864 the LNWR

Right **Garston Dock:** A rail tour calls at Garston Dock station on 6 June 1959. *Bevan Price*

Left **Garston Dock:** The site of the station in June 2005 – the same building can be seen in the 1959 picture. *Paul Wright*

Below **Garston Dock:** This is the station in the early 1960s. It is remarkably intact considering it has been closed to passengers since 1947. *Dave Nicholas*

made a connection with the Garston Dock line from its Speke Junction to Edge Hill Line. Shortly afterwards, on 29 July 1864, it absorbed the St Helens Canal & Railway Company.

The CLC ran trains to Manchester and beyond along the line using LNWR metals from Garston Dock eastwards. This never worked very well as the LNWR was not sympathetic to these services. On 1 August 1873 the CLC opened a direct line to Manchester, which began at Cressington Junction, just a short

distance to the west of Garston Dock station. The station was therefore no longer on the main line. However, the LNWR had opened a curve from Garston to Allerton on 1 January 1873, which now meant that a local service

L. M.& S. R. FOR CONDITIONS SEE BACK
MERCANTILE MARINE ON LEAVE

GARSTON DOCK TO

R.

Via

THIRD CLASS   497(S)MMoRL   Fare....s...d

062

Left **Garston Dock:** The station is seen here in June 1969 after the platforms had been demolished. *Nick Catford*

Below **Garston Dock:** A view of the station in 1922, looking north-west towards Liverpool Central. By this time passenger services did not travel towards Central. The LNWR operated a passenger service from Liverpool Lime Street that terminated at Garston Dock; trains came into the station from the south-east, having travelled around the Allerton curve. *Stations UK*

could operate from Garston Dock to Liverpool Lime Street. Trains now departed towards the east, turning north to reach the city whereas previously they had departed towards the west to reach Brunswick.

The station was provided with two platforms. Booking facilities were located on the eastbound platform and a substantial waiting shelter was provided on the westbound, although of course through passenger trains only used the station for nine years.

The local passenger service, established after 1873 and calling at all stations to Liverpool Lime Street, lasted until 16 June 1947, except for a brief period between 5 April 1917 and 5 May 1919 when the station was closed as a wartime economy measure.

For many years after closure the line was used as an important freight artery between Cressington Junction and points to the east, but it closed in the 1970s and today the site is occupied by a road.

MIDDLETON (1857)

Date opened:	1 May 1857
Location:	South side of Oldham Road, at the junction with Townley Street
Company on opening:	Lancashire & Yorkshire Railway
Date closed to passengers:	5 September 1964
Date closed completely:	1965
Company on closing:	British Railways (London Midland Region)
Present state:	Demolished – site occupied by industrial premises
County:	Lancashire (modern county of Greater Manchester)
OS Grid Ref:	SD874058

A line that would serve Middleton was first proposed by the Manchester & Leeds Railway, which wanted to build a line from its main line to Bury. Nothing came of this and it was not until 1854, when the Lancashire & Yorkshire Railway obtained an Act of Parliament, that work began. The line ran from a station called Mills Hill to a new terminus at Middleton.

Middleton station opened on 1 May 1857 and was provided with one short platform and basic booking facilities. By 1886 its original platform had been extended and it had been given a second platform. A substantial brick-built single-storey building was provided on the eastern side, with canopies on

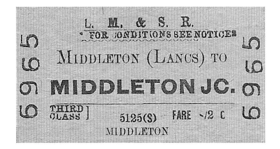

both platforms to protect passengers from the elements.

In the first published timetable there were nine trains per day in each direction, mostly running to Manchester Victoria. Within a few years services had built up to 19 arrivals and departures each day, with eight on Sunday. Excursion traffic was also popular, with 23 such workings organised for 1895.

Apart from the withdrawal of Sunday services in 1917 as a wartime economy measure (which were not reinstated after the end of hostilities), the pattern of frequent passenger services continued up to the end of the 1940s. By the 1960s services had been reduced to only six.

Although serving a fairly large town, Middleton station was unable to compete with high-frequency bus services that linked the town centre with Manchester, Rochdale and Oldham. The station closed officially

Top **Middleton:** A brake-van tour arrives at Middleton station in the 1960s. *Bevan Price*

Above **Middleton:** A view of the brake-van tour's locomotive at the buffer stops. *Bevan Price*

Left **Middleton:** This view shows the station site during the same brake-van tour. Amazingly the station was still open at this time, although its derelict condition would make many potential passengers think otherwise. *Bevan Price*

to passenger services on Monday 7 September 1964. However, the last scheduled passenger train had left on the 5th at 4.49pm for Manchester Victoria. Goods services continued to run until October 1965.

The Railway Hotel, on the north side of Oldham Road, is the only evidence that there was once a railway at this location. Overgrown sections of trackbed still exist about a mile south of the station site.

Above **Middleton:** Another view taken during the tour, looking towards the station. *Bevan Price*

Left **Middleton:** Looking south-east across Oldham Road towards the station site, the station entrance was on the corner of the Oldham Road /Townley Street road junction, behind the current 'Oldham Road' sign. A car park occupies the site of the buffer-stop end of the station. *Bevan Price*

Left **Middleton:** Looking south-east from Townley Street. The passenger station was on the left, while the lorries are on the site of former freight sidings between the station and St Michael's Church (just out of sight on the right). *Bevan Price*

RAINFORD JUNCTION (1858)
Ormskirk Platform

Date opened:	1 March 1858
Location:	At west end of Rainford Junction station on north side of Kirkby-Wigan Line
Company on opening:	Lancashire & Yorkshire Railway
Date closed to passengers:	5 November 1956
Date closed completely:	5 November 1956
Company on closing:	British Railways (London Midland Region)
Present state:	Platform still extant but heavily overgrown
County:	Lancashire (modern county of Merseyside)
OS Grid Ref:	SD476026

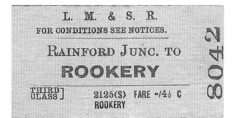

Rainford Junction: This is the Ormskirk platform looking west in the early part of the 21st century. A freight train is proceeding towards Wigan on the former LYR Liverpool to Wigan line. *Bevan Price*

Rainford Junction: This view looking west in 1949 gives a view of both the Ormskirk and St Helens platforms. The St Helens platform is to the left of the picture. At this time a service still ran from here to St Helens. *Stations UK*

RAINFORD JUNCTION St Helens Platform

Date opened:	1 February 1858
Location:	At west end of Rainford Junction station, on south side of Kirkby-Wigan line
Company on opening:	Lancashire & Yorkshire Railway
Date closed to passengers:	16 June 1951
Date closed completely:	16 June 1951
Company on closing:	British Railways (London Midland Region)
Present state:	Platform still extant but heavily overgrown
County:	Lancashire (modern county of Merseyside)
OS Grid Ref:	SD476025

Rainford Junction was built by the Lancashire & Yorkshire Railway as a replacement station for its existing facilities on the Liverpool Exchange to Wigan Line. The reason for the relocation was to facilitate interchange with both the St Helens Railway's line to St Helens, which opened on 1 February 1858, and the East Lancashire Railway's line to Ormskirk, which opened on 1 March of that year. Both lines came into the new station from a westerly direction, the St Helens line curving in from the south and the Ormskirk line from the north. A single-track link line was provided between the two lines, bypassing the station, but it was mostly used by goods services.

In order that the operation of the main line through Rainford Junction was not affected, a single platform was provided for the Ormskirk

Rainford Junction: The St Helens platform at Rainford Junction looking east in 1968. *Tony Graham*

Rainford Junction: The St Helens platform, looking south in February 2006. *Bevan Price*

Rainford Junction: The St Helens platform looking north, also in February 2006. *Bevan Price*

line. In effect it was a continuation of the eastbound (Wigan) platform, which stretched beyond the junction. Trains on Ormskirk services could thus terminate here without blocking the main line. Within a couple of years of opening, the Ormskirk line also became part of the Lancashire & Yorkshire Railway, so the company concentrated its booking facilities at in its own buildings on the eastbound platform.

By 1906 the LYR was operating 19 services per day to Ormskirk with a railmotor (11 on Sunday). In 1923 all of the lines into Rainford Junction became part of the LMS, but the pattern of services was not altered – trains still ran independently to St Helens and to Ormskirk, and passengers wishing to travel the entire length of the line had to change at Rainford Junction. By the 1930s the LMS had

replaced the railmotor on the Ormskirk service with a push-pull locomotive and a couple of coaches.

However, after 1945 passenger numbers declined and in 1951 all of the halts on the Ormskirk line and all of the St Helens line stations closed. The service to Ormskirk continued until 5 November 1956, and the line remained in use for goods services until1964.

Rainford Junction station is still open today, but was renamed Rainford in 1973. Part of the Ormskirk platform can still be seen at the end of the Wigan platform.

Rainford Junction: A view looking east from Rainford Junction signal box in 1976. The remains of the St Helens platform can clearly be seen to the right of the picture. *Tony Graham*

ROYTON (1864)

Date opened:	21 March 1864
Location:	South side of High Barn Street
Company on opening:	Lancashire & Yorkshire Railway
Date closed to passengers:	16 April 1966
Date closed completely:	16 April 1966
Company on closing:	British Railways (London Midland Region)
Present state:	Demolished – site now redeveloped as a residential area
County:	Lancashire (modern county of Greater Manchester)
OS Grid Ref:	SD922077

Royton station was the terminus of a short branch line that ran for just under 1¼ miles from the Lancashire & Yorkshire Railway's Oldham Mumps to Rochdale line. Royton was the only station on the line.

The line was opened primarily to serve the cotton-manufacturing town of Royton, which had been missed by the Oldham Mumps to Rochdale line. A single platform capable of accommodating an eight-coach train was located on the south side of the line, and a single-storey brick building provided the usual facilities. A canopy gave passengers shelter from the elements.

From the start the station was well served by passenger trains, mostly running from Manchester Victoria to Royton via Oldham. In 1922 18 services served the station every weekday. In 1923 the line became part of the

London Midland & Scottish Railway, which the following year considered the branch for electrification as part of a project to electrify many heavily used passenger lines in the Manchester area. However, the electrification project was never taken forward.

The station continued to be well served into the nationalisation period. In 1958 there were still up to 17 services each weekday, but Sunday services had ceased by this time. In the early 1960s British Railways introduced two-car DMUs, which proved very popular and even more passengers started to use the line.

Royton: This is the view looking south along the platform during a visit by the LCGB Middleton Branch Brake Van Tour on 7 August 1965. The station had lost its canopy by this time.
Bevan Price

At 6.12am on 8 February 1961 two empty
Cravens twin units, coupled together, ran into
the buffers at Royton station at 40mph. Having
demolished the buffer stops and the wall
behind them, the train dropped about 2 feet
to the level of High Barn Street and continued
across it, entering two houses and finally
coming to rest with its front end projecting
into their back yards. The leading bogie became
detached and fell into the cellar of one of the

Above **Royton:** On the same day
we are now looking north-west
towards the buffer stops. The
Railway Hotel is on the extreme
left, behind the gas lamp.
Bevan Price

Left **Royton:** On 16 April 1966,
the last day of public services, the
LCGB 'Cotton Pickers Railtour'
visited the station. Locomotive
No 47202 is running round ready
for departure. *Bevan Price*

houses. Damage was also caused to adjacent properties in the terraced row. Fortunately one of the properties was a lock-up shop, unoccupied at the time, and due to the early hour the occupants of the other houses were upstairs. It was concluded that the driver mishandled the brakes, as well as unwittingly accelerating the train, during the 1 in 62 decent to the station. Five people were injured.

Despite the heavy passenger use, the line was earmarked for closure. Goods services finished in 1964 and the last passenger service departed from Royton at 18.50 on 16 April 1966. Shortly afterwards the line was lifted and the station demolished.

Today the site has been developed as a residential area. The adjacent Railway Hotel is the sole remaining indication that a station existed at this location. However, about ¼ mile south from the station site the Shaw Road overbridge still exists, retained for use by a footpath along part of the trackbed towards Royton Junction.

Top **Royton:** Looking south-east towards the site of Royton station in December 2007. The houses follow the line of the platform and trackbed. *Bevan Price*

Centre **Royton:** Looking north-west from Shaw Road overbridge towards the site of the station in December 2007. *Bevan Price*

Right **Royton:** Shaw Road overbridge, looking south east in December 2007, part of trackbed here is now in use as a footpath *Bevan Price*

LIVERPOOL Brunswick (1864)

Date opened:	1 June1864
Location:	On the west side of Sefton Street
Company on opening:	Garston & Liverpool Railway
Date closed to passengers:	1 March 1874
Date closed completely:	1971
Company on closing:	Cheshire Lines Committee
Present state:	Station demolished – site occupied by a car dealership. The base of an original gatepost can still be seen, together with other remnants of the later goods facilities.
County:	Lancashire (modern county of Merseyside)
OS Grid Ref:	SJ349883

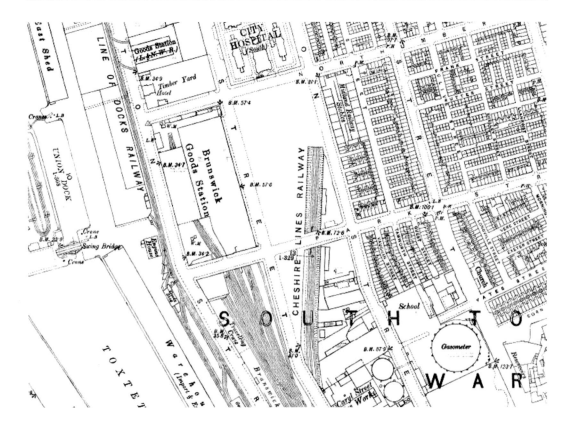

Brunswick station opened as the western terminus of the Garston & Liverpool Railway, which extended the St Helens Railway from Garston Dock to a point nearer the city at Brunswick. This line was opened on 1 June 1864, and just over a year later, on 5 July 1865, it was absorbed by the Cheshire Lines Committee (CLC).

The CLC had wanted a route into the important maritime city of Liverpool from the important manufacturing city of Manchester that could compete with the LNWR, and by obtaining running powers over the St Helens Railway and the Stockport & Warrington Railway it was able to achieve this. The problem was that both of these lines were subsequently taken over by the LNWR, and that company was not particularly inclined to be helpful towards the CLC.

The CLC therefore obtained powers to build its own line from a point just to the north-west of Garston Dock station to Manchester, and it opened on 1 August 1873. The CLC now had its own express route linking the two cities.

Brunswick station had extensive facilities, including a three-storey brick-built booking office. However, it was a mile from Liverpool city centre, but at the same time as the CLC had obtained powers for its main line to Manchester it had also obtained powers to build an extension into the city centre.

On 2 March 1874 the extension, complete with a new

Above **Liverpool Brunswick:** Brunswick station in the early 1960s. *Dave Nicholas*

Below left **Liverpool Brunswick:** Looking south-east towards the site of the station building. Note the base of the surviving gatepost. *Paul Wright*

Below Liverpool Brunswick: A surviving gatepost from the entrance to Brunswick station in June 2006. *Paul Wright*

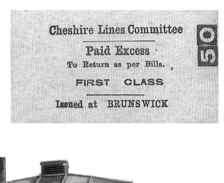

terminus called Liverpool Central, was opened, and Brunswick closed the next day. However, that was not the end of the story as the station was developed into an extensive goods facility, including a large warehouse that stood right next to the original station building.

It is known that troop trains used Brunswick station during the Liverpool General Transport Strike of 1911. This was presumably to avoid the mass demonstrations that would have been present outside Liverpool Central station. It was probably also easier to unload the horses of the Cavalry detachments at the extensive goods facilities that Brunswick had at that time. The goods facilities remained in use until the early 1970s.

Today the site is occupied by a large car dealership, but the base of one of the original station gateposts can still be seen.

Right **Liverpool Brunswick:** A view looking east at the approach lines to the station in 1950. At that time Brunswick was an important goods station.
Stations UK

HORWICH (1870)

Date opened:	14 February 1870
Location:	South side of Church Street
Company on opening:	Lancashire & Yorkshire Railway
Date closed to passengers:	27 September 1965
Date closed completely:	1966
Company on closing:	British Railways (London Midland Region)
Present state:	Demolished – site now redeveloped as a residential area and public park
County:	Lancashire (modern county of Greater Manchester)
OS Grid Ref:	SD640115

Horwich station was opened by the Lancashire & Yorkshire Railway on 14 February 1870, and was located at the end of a 1¼-mile branch from the LYR Bolton to Preston line. The station was provided with one platform and a single-storey brick building that provided the usual facilities. Extensive goods sidings were also provided.

In 1884 the LYR chose Horwich as a suitable location for a railway works. In 1886 the works took in its first locomotives for repair, but over the following decades it expanded

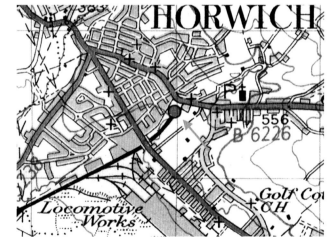

Left **Horwich:** A view looking south at Horwich station during a visit by a rail tour in the 1960s. *Bevan Price*

until, by the 1890s, it employed more than 5,000 men and boys.

The opening of the works brought much custom to Horwich station, from which trains ran to Bolton and to Manchester, although outside peak hours most services ran as a shuttle to Blackrod on the main line. For a period up to 1943 the shuttle service was provided by a railmotor, which became known locally as 'Blackrod Jerk'. By the 1950s most of the passengers using the station were employees of the railway works, who travelled on privilege tickets. In 1961 the station was proposed for closure, and regular passenger services ceased on 27 September 1965, the last train being the 12.05pm to Bolton. The station remained in use for goods services until 1966.

The railway works finally closed in 1983, and today a public park stands on the site of the railway station.

Top right **Horwich:** A September 2005 view looking south from a similar viewpoint as the 1960s picture. *Paul Wright*

Centre right **Horwich:** The original pedestrian entrance to Horwich station in September 2008. *Paul Wright*

Right **Horwich:** A view looking north at the station site in September 2008. It is now a public park called 'Old Station Park'. *Paul Wright*

CANADA DOCK (1870)

Date opened:	1 July 1870
Location:	Between Derby Road and Bankhall Lane
Company on opening:	London & North Western Railway
Date closed to passengers:	5 May 1941
Date closed completely:	12 September 1982
Company on closing:	London & North Western Railway
Present state:	Demolished – site has been filled in
County:	Lancashire (modern county of Merseyside)
OS Grid Ref:	SJ342936

Canada Dock station was situated on the LNWR's Canada Dock branch, which ran from Edge Hill through the northern suburbs of Liverpool to the Docks. The line opened to Canada Dock in 1866 for goods traffic and as far as Tue Brook for passenger services. In 1870 a passenger service was extended along the line to a single-platform terminus at Canada Dock, which at the time of opening was called Bootle. The station was renamed Canada Dock on 5 September 1881.

The station had a long single platform below street level, and a set of wooden steps led up to a single-storey brick-built booking hall on Derby Road. From the beginning train services ran between Canada Dock station and Liverpool Lime Street in the city centre. To reach their destination trains took a circuitous route through the outer suburbs of the city. A very large goods yard completely surrounded the station.

The station served dock workers well for many years but by 1932 there were only five weekday arrivals and five departures, with a long gap in the service during the daytime. In May 1941 the site was severely damaged in an enemy air raid, and the passenger station never reopened. The goods yard did reopen and it remained in use until 1982. Remarkably the station platform and building survived intact until the 1990s.

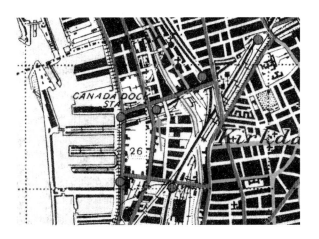

Today the site has been filled in and only some different-coloured brickwork in a wall shows the location of the booking office.

Right **Canada Dock:** A rail tour arrives at Canada Dock station on 6 June 1959.
Bevan Price

Below **Canada Dock:** An view of the station from a high elevation in 1977, when it was still in use as a goods station.
Derek Knowler

Bottom **Canada Dock:** The station in 1990.
Paul Wright

Top right **Canada Dock:** The site of the station in September 2005. Note the different brickwork in the wall – that is where the booking office was located. This picture is from a similar viewpoint to the 1990 picture, but the levels are completely different as the site has been filled in. *Paul Wright*

Centre right **Canada Dock:** This is the station in February 1986, only four years after it had closed to goods services. *Martin Brown*

Below **Canada Dock:** A view looking east along the single platform in the 1930s. The station was surrounded by goods facilities, which were always busier than the passenger station. *Stations UK*

WINSFORD & OVER (1870)

Date opened:	1 July 1870
Location:	North side of junction of Over Lane and Church Street
Company on opening:	Cheshire Lines Committee
Date closed to passengers:	1 June 1931
Date closed completely:	1 September 1958
Company on closing:	Cheshire Lines Committee
Present state:	Demolished
County:	Cheshire
OS Grid Ref:	SJ665655

The CLC's Winsford & Over branch opened on 1 July 1870 to give access to the numerous salt works in the Winsford area. One of only two stations on the line, it was a single-platform terminus with substantial goods facilities. It opened for passenger business on 1 January 1874, but closed a few years later on 1 January 1874, only to reopen 12 years later on 1 May 1886. A further period of closure followed

Winsford & Over: A view looking towards the buffer stops in 1950. The station's basic facilities can clearly be seen. *Stations UK*

between 1 December 1888 and 1 February 1892, following which was the station's longest period of continuous business, lasting until final closure on 1 January 1931.

The branch continued in use as goods line, which had always been its primary purpose, until the early 1960s. The goods service

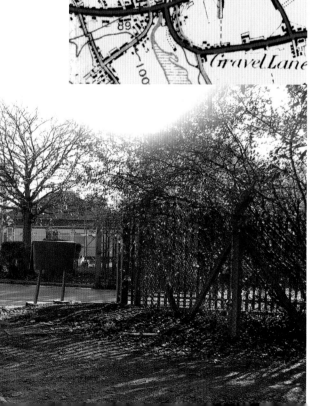

Above **Winsford & Over:** Looking north from the site of the station in November 2005. *Paul Wright*

Below **Winsford & Over:** Looking south from the site, also in November 2005. *Paul Wright*

Winsford & Over: A sign at the beginning of the 'Whitegate Way', a short distance to the north of the station site on the old trackbed. *Paul Wright*

was withdrawn from Winsford & Over in 1958, but was retained at Whitegate until 1963. Today the site of the station is occupied by a small industrial estate, but the route of the line is a popular footpath and bridleway called the 'Whitegate Way'.

LIVERPOOL Central (High Level) (1874)

Date opened:	2 March 1874
Location:	Junction of Ranelagh Place and Bold Street
Company on opening:	Cheshire Lines Committee
Date closed to passengers:	17 April 1972
Date closed completely:	17 April 1972
Company on closing:	British Rail (London Midland Region)
Present state:	Extensive sections of the station's walls can still be seen behind the present Central station
County:	Lancashire (modern county of Merseyside)
OS Grid Ref:	SJ350902

Liverpool Central station opened as part of the Cheshire Lines Committee's extension of its Liverpool and Manchester line into Liverpool's city centre, having previously terminated at the inconveniently located Brunswick station (qv). The line that ran from Brunswick was entirely in tunnels or cuttings until it reached Central station.

Being a relative latecomer to Liverpool, the CLC had to make do with a very cramped site. Nevertheless it built an imposing station with a grand three-storey fa ade behind which was a single arched trainshed that reached a height of 65 feet. The station had three island platforms giving six platform faces.

By 1880 the CLC was offering the fastest journey times between Liverpool and Manchester, at 45 minutes for the 34-mile journey. By 1883 this had been reduced to 40 minutes. Within a few years of its opening Central station offered services to Manchester, Stockport,

Southport and shorter all-stations workings along these routes. It also offered, through the constituent parts of the CLC, journeys further afield. The GNR ran services to Hull, Harwich and London Marylebone, while the Midland ran services to London St Pancras.

On 11 January 1892 the Mersey Railway opened low-level platforms at Central station,

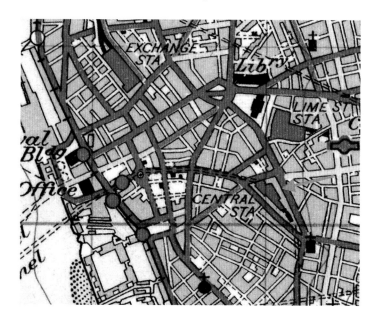

which catered for its services that ran deep beneath the River Mersey to Rock Ferry and Birkenhead. This made Liverpool Central an even busier place, as interchange opportunities were very good.

In 1923, at the time of the Grouping, the CLC was left as an independent company, but its shares were split between the LNER (two-thirds) and the LMS (one-third). The CLC had never owned any locomotives itself – these had always been provided by the parent companies. After 1923 LNER types were the most dominant. Services still ran to both London Marylebone (LNER) and St Pancras (LMS), but the LMS tended to concentrate its London services on the route from nearby Liverpool Lime Street.

The station remained busy throughout the period from 1923 and well into the nationalisation era. In 1960 daily departures were listed to Aintree Central, Gateacre, Harwich Parkeston Quay, Hull, Hunts Cross, Leicester Central, London Marylebone, Manchester Central, Nottingham Victoria, Stockport Tiviot Dale, Tanhouse Lane and Warrington Central. However, despite this level of traffic Central was listed for closure under the Beeching report, as most of its

Above **Liverpool Central:** The high-level station in seen here in June 1969, looking towards the buffer stops. *Nick Catford*

services could be rerouted into Lime Street via the Allerton Curve. This duly happened in September 1966, but it was not to be the end of the station – it was kept open to serve the hourly Gateacre service.

Above **Liverpool Central:** Another view in June 1969, by which time part of the station had become a car park. The former Mersey Railway underground platform was located beneath the cars. *Nick Catford*

In its later years the high-level platforms at Central were a sad spectacle. Only two running lines were left in situ, one on each side of one of the island platforms. Other than the concourse, which provided access to the low-level platforms and remained busy, the rest of the station took on a derelict air.

By the early 1970s the station site was needed as a construction base for the planned Merseyrail loop and link underground system. On 17 April 1972 the Gateacre service ended and the high-level platforms at Central closed for good. On 28 July 1975 the low-level platforms also closed, but for them it was only a temporary measure as they reopened on 9 May 1977 as part of the new link line

forming the cross-city section of the Merseyrail Northern Line. New deep-level platforms were also opened to cater for the former Mersey Railway service, by then the Merseyrail Wirral line.

In January 1978 the original route east out of Liverpool Central high level also reopened, but it was excavated out a few hundred metres from the end of the original platforms to allow trains to drop down to the low-level platforms.

Today various parts of the high-level station can still be seen, as much of the site is a public car park. This will not last for long, however, as the whole site is earmarked for a shopping development. The 'Central' name lives on through the Merseyrail station that occupies the same site, although trains are now relegated to below the streets. On a brighter note, the modern Central station is probably as busy as it ever was.

BOLTON Great Moor Street (1874)

Date opened:	28 September 1874
Location:	South side of Great Moor Street at junction with Black Horse Street
Company on opening:	London & North Western Railway
Date closed to passengers:	29 March 1954
Date closed completely:	1958?
Company on closing:	British Railways (London Midland Region)
Present state:	Demolished – site cleared and partly redeveloped
County:	Lancashire (modern county of Greater Manchester)
OS Grid Ref:	SD716088

Bolton Great Moor Street was situated at the end of the line from Kenyon Junction, which had opened in stages from 1828 to 1831 as the Bolton & Leigh Railway; the first section, from Bolton to Chequerbent, opened on 28 August 1828. The line was engineered by George Stephenson and it was one of his locomotives, *Lancashire Witch*, that made the inaugural run. The line had reached Leigh by March 1830 but it was not until 2 June 1831, when it reached Kenyon Junction on the famous Liverpool & Manchester Railway, that passenger services began. The first passenger

run was an excursion from Bolton to Newton for a horse-racing event.

Early station facilities at Bolton would have been quite basic, and a service of two trains per day to Liverpool began on 13 June 1831.

A new enlarged station opened in 1867 to replace the first station at Great Moor Street, which was nearby but at a lower level. In 1874 it was completely rebuilt in a classic 'Italian' style, the station and its approaches being on a viaduct. The station consisted of four platform faces 300 feet long, covered by a roof and provided with extensive waiting facilities. The

Left **Bolton Great Moor Street:** The site of the station in May 2006. The entrance was on Great Moor Street, to the left of the traffic lights. The station lay roughly parallel to Black Horse Street, with the approach viaduct lying in the area now occupied by the supermarkets that can just be seen in the distance. *Bevan Price*

Bolton Great Moor Street:
This is the station during a visit by
a rail tour in 1963. *Bevan Price*

rebuild had come about as a new direct line
to Manchester had been authorised, which
would allow the LNWR, by this time the
owning company, to compete with the LYR,
which had a direct line between Bolton and
Manchester. The direct line opened from
Great Moor Street to Roe Green on 1 April
1875.

By the mid-1930s more than 20 services
operated from Great Moor Street along the
Kenyon Junction line, with fewer but still
significant services along the Manchester line.

After nationalisation in 1948 the value of
having two lines from Manchester to Bolton
was being questioned. The Great Moor Street
service took longer than the former LYR
route, and by 1954 only four trains a day
operated towards Manchester. The Kenyon
Junction line had also declined, and only six
trains operated to either Kenyon Junction or
Warrington. All regular services operating out
of Bolton Great Moor Street ceased on 27
March 1954, the last train being the 10.35pm to
Kenyon Junction.

After closure, Rugby League specials and
holiday trains continued to use the station until

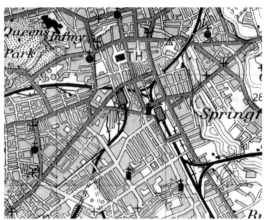

1958, and goods traffic continued until the
early 1960s. The Manchester direct line was
the first to be lifted, then the Kenyon line was
lifted in stages between 1963 and 1969, the
southernmost section surviving the longest.

Bolton Great Moor Street station was
demolished in 1966 and replaced with a leisure
pool, which was itself demolished in 2003.

Today there are no traces of the station
and the site has been partially redeveloped.

CHESTER Northgate (1875)

Date opened:	I May 1875
Location:	East side of Victoria Road
Company on opening:	Cheshire Lines Committee
Date closed to passengers:	6 October 1969
Date closed completely:	6 October 1969
Company on closing:	British Rail (London Midland Region)
Present state:	Demolished – now the site of a sports centre
County:	Cheshire
OS Grid Ref:	SJ405669

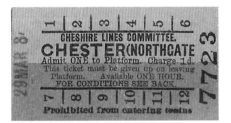

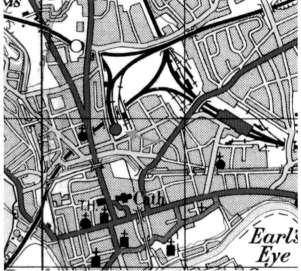

Chester Northgate station was the CLC's terminus in Cheshire's county town. Situated close to the city's historic 'North Gate', the CLC line turned to the east and headed off towards Northwich and on to Manchester. On 31 March 1890 a further line was opened by the Manchester, Sheffield & Lincolnshire Railway (later the Great Central Railway), which headed west to Hawarden Bridge. Later extensions saw this line reach Wrexham and Birkenhead. An avoiding line was also built so that trains could pass from east to west through Chester without having to terminate at Chester Northgate. This created a triangle of lines to the north of the station.

The station was provided with two lengthy platforms, covered by an overall roof at their south end. The main facilities were provided on the west side of the station. By the early

20th century typical train services ran to destinations such as Manchester Central, Wrexham Central and Seacombe.

In its later years the station's overall roof was reduced to cover only the western platform, but new waiting facilities were provided on the east side to compensate.

Well into the 1960s trains continued to serve destinations such as Wrexham, New Brighton and Manchester. Lines heading out of the station to the west were the first to lose their passenger services in September 1968, leaving only the Manchester Central service. A connection was installed between the CLC line and the former Birkenhead Joint Line at Mickle

Above **Chester Northgate:** The station is seen in October 1969; a Manchester DMU is about to depart. *Bevan Price*

Below left **Chester Northgate:** A view from the buffer stops in October 1969. *Bevan Price*

MAY 1948
C. L. C.   FOR CONDITIONS SEE BACK
Valid on day of issue only
PARKING TICKET FOR
CHARABANC
AT
CHESTER (NORTHGATE)
Registration No ....
Fee 10/· Z

Right **Chester Northgate:**
Looking north from the site of
the station in April 2005.
Paul Wright

Below **Chester Northgate:** The
site of Northgate station looking
north, also in April 2005.
Paul Wright

Trafford, which allowed Manchester trains
to be diverted to Chester General, and soon
afterwards, on 6 October 1969, Northgate
station closed. The site was redeveloped and
today is occupied by a Leisure Centre called
Northgate Arena.

The avoiding line continued in use for a few
years as a goods line, before closing on 20 April
1984. It was reopened as a single-track line on
31 August 1986, but was closed again by the
early 1990s, after which it was mothballed for a
while, then lifted.

BIRKENHEAD Woodside (1878)

Date opened:	31 March 1878
Location:	Chester Street
Company on opening:	Great Western Railway and London & North Western Railway
Date closed to passengers:	5 November 1967
Date closed completely:	5 November 1967
Company on closing:	British Rail (London Midland Region)
Present state:	Demolished, but sections of side walls remain
County:	Cheshire (modern county of Merseyside)
OS Grid Ref:	SJ329893

Birkenhead Woodside Station opened on 31 March 1878 as a replacement for an earlier terminus at Monks Ferry which had opened on 23 October 1844. The station was located right next to the Ferry Terminal for Liverpool so in effect it served that city even though it was located in Birkenhead. It was built further inland than originally conceived, in order to avoid demolition of the Mersey ferries workshop, situated on the bank of the river. In order to join up with the existing track of the Chester & Birkenhead Railway, a half-mile-long tunnel from Woodside to a point alongside the existing Monks Ferry tunnel entrance, near Grange Lane, was constructed using cut-and-cover.

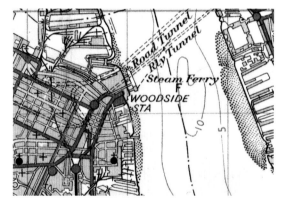

The station was a grandiose building, with two semi-cylindrical roofs covering much of the platforms. However, given the size of the station, it only had five short (but wide) platforms, as much of the space was taken up by middle tracks and a roadway.

The station building was known to local rail users as 'the wrong way round', because for the majority of the station's life its original rear entrance was used as the main booking hall, whereas Woodside's 'front' entrance was mainly used for handling parcels. This entrance, covered in a porte-cochère to allow travelling gentry to avoid inclement weather, faced the graving dock on the south side of the station. It had been intended that passengers disembarking from the nearby ferry terminal of the same name would use this entrance. Unfortunately, the ferry companies were slow at co-operating and when the tram terminus opened in front of the ferry terminal in the early 1900s, the decision was made to keep the small 'back' entrance a permanent fixture. This was very unfortunate, as passengers arriving at the station never got to see the huge sandstone fireplaces, decorative brickwork and massive timber roof trusses holding up the roof of the intended booking hall.

Top **Birkenhead Woodside:**
A specially turned-out GWR-
liveried locomotive arrives at
Birkenhead Woodside in 1967.
Bevan Price

Centre and bottom **Birkenhead
Woodside:** The same train
is seen again from the other
direction and the same location
is captured in March 2005. *Bevan
Price/Paul Wright*

From early days the GWR
operated express trains to
London Paddington and these
continued right up to the
closure of the station. Other
services went to Chester,
North Wales, West Kirby and
Warrington. Routes further
afield included Great Western
Railway services to Chester
General, Wolverhampton
Low Level, Birmingham Snow
Hill, Shrewsbury General and
London Paddington. There
was even a service that went
to Liverpool Lime Street only
a couple of miles away across
the river but nearly 40 miles
by rail.

The station was very busy
right up to nationalisation.
However, as with many
other stations and rail
routes in Britain Dr Richard
Beeching, found the terminus
superfluous, as most of the
routes served could also be
taken from Liverpool Lime
Street station, on the other
side of the River Mersey.

By early 1967 there were
still six through trains on
weekdays between Birkenhead
Woodside and London Paddington. In March of
that year the route was effectively curtailed at
Wolverhampton, as a result of the introduction
of electric trains on the West Coast Main Line.
At the same time, the last steam service left the
station with the withdrawal of through services
to Birmingham.

Only the hourly diesel train service to
Chester and trains to Helsby remained to use
the station. With the curtailment of these at
Rock Ferry, the station closed to passengers on
5 November 1967 and was demolished within a
couple of years.

Birkenhead Woodside was a typical example
of a busy station axed because it served

destinations that Liverpool Lime Street also served. Today most of the lines that led up to Woodside are as busy as ever but they are connected into the former Mersey Railway as part of the Merseyrail network. Chester can still be reached from Woodside as Hamilton Square underground station is situated just across the square.

Today, the only evidence of its existence is part of the station wall, a road bridge and the tunnel, which lay at the station throat. The gates of the station were reused at a house in Gayton. The rest of the land is now used as a bus depot.

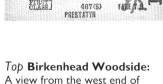

Top **Birkenhead Woodside:** A view from the west end of the station in 1967, as a London Paddington train waits to depart. *Bevan Price*

Above **Birkenhead Woodside:** Surviving floor tiles from the concourse in 1986. *Michael Rymill*

Left **Birkenhead Woodside:** This surviving section of the station's outer wall was photographed on 6 February 2005. *Paul Wright*

Bottom of page **Birkenhead Woodside:** A view looking east towards the ferry terminal at Birkenhead Woodside in the 1950s; the station can be seen on the right of the picture. *Stations UK*

MANCHESTER Central (1880)

Date opened:	1 July 1880
Location:	South side of Windmill Street
Company on opening:	Cheshire Lines Committee
Date closed to passengers:	5 May 1969
Date closed completely:	5 May 1969
Company on closing:	British Rail (London Midland Region)
Present state:	Station building still standing, now the 'Central' exhibition hall
County:	Lancashire (modern county of Greater Manchester)
OS Grid Ref:	SJ837977

Manchester Central station was opened by the Cheshire Lines Committee (CLC) on 1 July 1880. The CLC was a partnership of three railway companies that had come together in the 1860s: the Great Northern Railway, the Manchester, Sheffield & Lincolnshire Railway, and the Midland Railway.

The CLC partners had all gained access to Manchester by the end of the 1860s through a variety of agreements that involved running over the lines of other companies. The MS&LR shared a terminus station with the London & North Western Railway at Manchester London

Road, and allowed the Midland and the GNR to use its part of the station. However, by the 1870s this situation was becoming a problem as

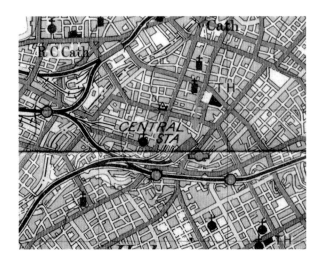

London Road was increasingly congested. Outright hostility to the MR on the part of the LNWR did not help matters.

With the opening of the CLC main line from Liverpool to Manchester in 1873, and its purpose-built terminus station at Liverpool Central on 2 March 1874, the need for a station in central Manchester became even more pressing. The CLC had to run its trains from Liverpool and from its mid-Cheshire line into Manchester London Road, which once again meant that there was a reliance on the LNWR.

In June 1872 the CLC obtained an Act that granted it powers to extend its line from Liverpool into central Manchester and create a terminus station of its own. On 9 July 1877 a station known as Manchester Central opened at Windmill Street at the back of the city's Free Trade Hall. This station was destined to have only a very short life, as at the time of its opening work was well under way on its permanent replacement.

The CLC chose its resident engineer, Mr Lewis Henry Moorsom, to build its permanent Manchester Central station and work on the building commenced in 1875. Notorious slum dwellings, which had inspired the writings of

Above **Manchester Central:** A side view of the station in February 2005. *Paul Wright*

Below **Manchester Central:** Another view of the station in February 2005. *Paul Wright*

Friedrich Engels, occupied the land on which the station was to be built, and the City Fathers were pleased to see the area cleared, although it is doubtful that any thought would have been given to the individuals who lived there. Robert Neill & Sons undertook the construction work at a cost of £124,778.

During the construction of the station the MR found a way of accessing it from its main line to London St Pancras. In January 1876 the MS&LR had given the MR notice to quit Manchester London Road station within three years.

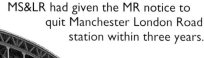

Above **Manchester Central:** The south side of Manchester Central in February 2005. *Paul Wright*

The MR therefore took over a project that had been proposed by the Manchester South District Railway in 1873, obtained its own Act to build the line in July 1877, and started work on it in 1878. The line connected the CLC Liverpool to Manchester route, just over a mile to the west of Manchester Central near Cornbrook, with the CLC Glazebrook to Woodley route via Stockport Tiviot Dale at Heaton Mersey, thus giving the MR a route into Central Station.

When the station opened it consisted of a magnificent single-span arched roof, constructed by Andrew Handyside & Co; it was 210 feet wide and 550 feet long, with a maximum height of 90 feet. The frame weighed 2,400 tons and was covered with a combination of slate and glass. Beneath the roof there were six platform faces, four of which were provided by two island platforms. The platforms were served by nine tracks, the extra lines being used by engines to run round their trains. The running lines and platforms were above street level and

beneath them were huge brick-built cellars that could be used to store goods. The lines exited the station via some very heavily engineered bridges and viaducts, which carried the line down to Cornbrook were the Liverpool, Heaton Mersey and Chester lines separated.

The main public entrance to the station was at the Windmill Street end. At the time of opening wooden buildings provided all of the usual facilities, including the main booking office. These facilities were meant to be a temporary measure, as it was intended that a hotel would be constructed to form a grand frontage to the station. A large clock was provided on the inside and outside of the station. When the permanent station opened, its temporary predecessor closed to passengers and was developed as a goods station.

From the opening of Manchester Central, trains ran to Liverpool via the CLC main line, to Stockport and beyond via the South District line and to Northwich and Chester via the CLC's

Below **Manchester Central:** A local train service departs from Manchester Central station in 1957. The picture illustrates just how busy this city centre terminus once was. At this time the station was still served by numerous long-distance services and a plethora of suburban commuter trains. *H. C. Casseley*

Above **Manchester Central:** A view of the station in 1975 when it was in a very derelict state and in use as a car park. *Tony Doherty*

mid-Cheshire route. From Monday 2 August 1880 the MR began to run express services between Manchester Central and Buxton, Derby and London St Pancras. From October 1891 the GNR started to run express trains between Manchester Central and London King's Cross; it had opened a new line that ran from Fairfield on the MS&LR main line between Manchester and Sheffield, to Chorlton-cum-Hardy, on the South District line, giving the company access to Central station. At the same time a local all-stations service was introduced between Manchester Central and Guide Bridge.

On 1 July 1897 the MS&LR changed its name to the Great Central Railway, and a couple of years later, on 15 March 1899, it opened its London Extension to Marylebone. From this date trains therefore also ran between the new GCR London terminus and Manchester Central.

In 1896 the MR purchased land at the front of Manchester Central station on which to build a hotel. By this time, however, it was decided that the hotel would not be built at the front of the station as originally envisaged, but a short distance away on the other side of Windmill Street. The hotel was designed by the MR's architect, Charles Trubshaw, assisted by William Towle. It was a magnificent structure, took four years to build, and was the height of luxury when it opened on 5 September 1903. A covered walkway was built between the station entrance and the hotel so that passengers could be protected from wet weather. The station's so-called temporary wooden buildings were destined to remain in place.

By the time the hotel opened passengers were able to travel between Manchester Central and Buxton, Chester Northgate, Derby, Hull, Liverpool Central, London King's Cross, London Marylebone, London St Pancras, Nottingham and Southport Lord Street. Local services radiated out to the south Manchester suburbs and to towns such as Warrington and Wigan. Because of the intense levels of traffic, the station had to be extended. In 1906 extra platforms were built outside the overall roof on the south-east side; they were constructed from wood and were provided with awnings to protect passengers from the elements. Three platform faces were created in all, one of which, platform 7, was effectively a bay at the end of platform 6. The new platforms were numbered 7, 8 and 9.

During the early years of the 20th century the MR made substantial investments to speed up its services from Manchester to London in direct competition with the LNWR. With the construction of a new direct line between Heaton Mersey and New Mills, which opened in 1902, MR express trains were reaching London from Manchester Central in 3hr 40min, which was only 10 minutes slower than the LNWR. The MR also provided levels of comfort, including the introduction of Pullman coaches, not previously seen in Britain.

In 1923 the GCR and the GNR became part of the London & North Eastern Railway while the MR became part of the London Midland & Scottish Railway. The CLC remained independent, but it now had only two partners, the LMS and the LNER; the latter had two-thirds of the shares and the LMS one-third.

After 1923 competition between the former LNWR and MR routes was no longer an issue as they both formed part of the LMS. Express services out of Manchester Central did not suffer, however, as the LMS considered the MR route to be important as it took pressure off the former LNWR line. During the 1930s two of the services between London St Pancras and Manchester Central were named, the 'Peak Express' and the 'Palatine'. The former covered the journey in 3hr 35min.

In 1935 the signalling at Manchester Central was modernised using the latest technology. Colour light signals replaced the semaphore signals that had served the station since its earliest days.

During the Second World War passenger services were reduced in number and saw a reduction in speed. At the end of hostilities it took many years for timings to reach anything like their pre-war levels.

From 1 January 1948 Manchester Central became part of the nationalised British Railways

Above **Manchester Central:** A view from the position of the station clock, looking down at the empty platforms in 1975. *Tony Doherty*

(London Midland Region), and the CLC was no more. In the early 1950s service patterns from Central were fairly familiar, but competition from road was having an effect on some of the more local services. The South District services, which at that time were running between Manchester Central and Stockport Tiviot Dale or Cheadle Heath, and which had once built up to a 10-minute frequency, were down to 23 per weekday by 1954. In 1952 the Southport Lord Street service was cut back to Aintree, and in July 1958 the Guide Bridge service ended.

A regular service between Liverpool Central and Manchester Central continued to run, and from 1958 the latter found itself handling an increase in express services to the south. This was because British Railways had decided to electrify the former LNWR route from Manchester London Road, which was renamed Manchester Piccadilly, to London Euston, and as the electrification work would cause delays it was decided to concentrate services at Manchester Central.

From 4 July 1960 a new train developed by British Railways, a diesel Pullman, which became known as the 'Blue Pullman', began to operate between Manchester Central and London St Pancras. The train was both modern and luxurious, completed the journey in 3hr 13min,

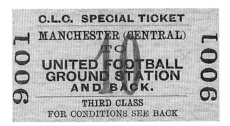

C.L.C. SPECIAL TICKET
MANCHESTER (CENTRAL)
TO
UNITED FOOTBALL
GROUND STATION
AND BACK.
THIRD CLASS
FOR CONDITIONS SEE BACK

and proved very popular with business travellers. Sleeping car services were also concentrated into Manchester Central at this time, but were routed over the former GCR main line to London Marylebone. Also in 1960 new four-car DMUs were introduced onto the Liverpool service. In 1961 DMUs also started to operate on the South District line and on services to Chester and Buxton. However, despite the modernisation steam-hauled services could still be seen at Manchester Central during this period.

The years between 1960 and 1966 were very busy at Manchester Central, but they were to prove to be a swansong. In April 1966 the electrification of the former LNWR route was completed and services were concentrated on that route. The 'Blue Pullman' ceased to operate in 1966, and on 1 January 1967 the South District service ended. As early as September 1966 British Rail, as it had then become known, was considering how it might close Manchester Central and divert the remaining services. A target date for closure was eventually set for June 1968, with an estimated cost of £539,000 – these costs were associated with the junction remodelling required to allow Liverpool and Chester trains to run towards Piccadilly.

From 1 January 1968 express services were diverted to run into Manchester Piccadilly, and the last expresses had run between Central and Nottingham and London St Pancras. From this date the only trains that served Manchester Central were the Liverpool and Chester services, together with a Sundays-only service that ran between Liverpool Lime Street and Sheffield Midland.

The closure date of June 1968 was not met, and a new date was set, 5 May 1969. The last trains left the station on Saturday 3 May 1969, and following its closure it was sold to the NCP Car Parking empire in 1972. It slowly decayed, acting not only as a symbol of the decline of Britain's railways but also of the country's industrial northern towns. In 1978 it was purchased by Greater Manchester Council, and thankfully, as Manchester began to resurrect itself from its decline in the early 1980s, the city officials focussed their attention on the station. In 1983 it was given listed status, then work began on converting it into an exhibition hall. On 7 March 1986 it reopened to the public as the GMEX exhibition hall, and for more than 20 years it hosted shows, exhibitions and concerts. In January 2007 the venue was renamed Manchester Central, once again taking on its historic name.

Below **Manchester Central:** Inside the trainshed at Manchester Central in October 1968. *Robin Lush*

HUSKISSON (1880)

Date opened:	13 July 1880
Location:	North side of Boundary Road
Company on opening:	Cheshire Lines Committee
Date closed to passengers:	1 May 1885
Date closed completely:	August 1975
Company on closing:	Cheshire Lines Committee
Present state:	Demolished
County:	Lancashire (modern county of Merseyside)
OS Grid Ref:	SJ344925

Huskisson station was situated on the Cheshire Lines Committee's North Liverpool Extension Line, which connected its main Liverpool to Manchester line to the north Liverpool Docks by skirting through agricultural land to the east of Liverpool. When the line first opened Walton-on-the-Hill was the terminus, but seven months later, on 13 July 1880, services started running through to Huskisson, which was close to the north Liverpool Docks.

The station consisted of an island platform, giving two platform faces, and was provided with a substantial roof canopy. Train services operated to both Liverpool Central and Manchester Central, and a large goods station was also opened adjacent to the passenger facilities.

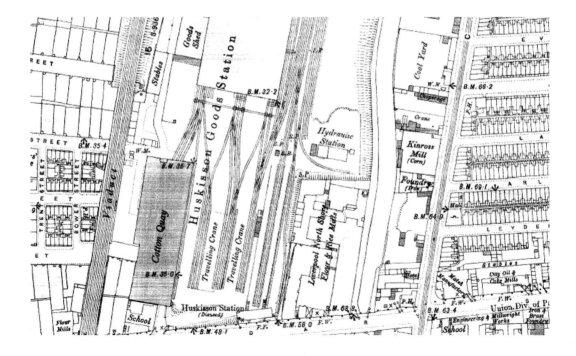

Services were not very well used and the passenger station closed on 13 July 1885, with services once again terminating at Walton-on-the-Hill, but only until 1912 when even that station closed for good. Huskisson's passenger station was converted for goods use, as space was desperately needed, and it remained open for railborne goods until August 1975, and for road services for some years after that.

Above **Huskisson:** A view looking south in 1954. The station is remarkably intact considering that it has been closed for nearly 70 years. *Stations UK*

Below **Huskisson:** The site of the station in August 2005. *Paul Wright*

ALEXANDRA DOCK (1881)

Date opened:	5 September 1881
Location:	Regent Road
Company on opening:	London & North Western Railway
Date closed to passengers:	31 May 1948
Date closed completely:	31 May 1948
Company on closing:	British Railways (London Midland Region)
Present state:	Demolished. The site of the station was at one time accessible as it was on a public road, but several years ago the Port of Liverpool sought a road closure and now the site is within the dock estate. It can be seen from Derby Road quite easily.
County:	Lancashire (modern county of Merseyside)
OS Grid Ref:	SJ335948

Alexandra Dock station was the terminus of the relatively short branch from the LNWR's Canada Dock branch (opened in 1866) at Atlantic Dock Junction, which was located in a deep cutting at the rear of the LYR's Bank Hall MPD. The branch opened on 5 September 1881, with stations at Balliol Road and Alexandra Dock.

When it opened the station was named 'Atlantic Dock', but it was renamed five days later on 10 September 1881 to Alexandra Dock, the name it kept until closure. It was a single-platform terminus with an overall roof. Its booking office was located on

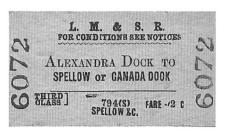

Liverpool's busy Dock Road (although its correct name was always Regent Road at this point), and confusingly there was another station called Alexandra Dock a short walk away on the Liverpool Overhead Railway.

Throughout its life Alexandra Dock station was served by local services that started at

Liverpool Lime Street, then called at all stations along the Canada Dock branch before turning north at Atlantic Dock Junction and heading for the terminus at Alexandra Dock. The LMS summer timetable for 1932 shows 13 arrivals at Alexandra Dock and 12 departures. This service finished on 31 May 1948 only five months into the nationalisation period.

The line was always more busy with freight, and remains so to this day, as it serves the north Liverpool Docks.

Above right **Alexandra Dock:** A view taken inside the trainshed after closure, during a visit by a rail tour on 6 June 1959. *Bevan Price*

Right **Alexandra Dock:** The same rail tour prepares to leave Alexandra Dock station. *Bevan Price*

Below **Alexandra Dock:** A view of the site of the station looking west from Derby Road Bridge on 19 June 2005. The station was situated roughly where the present tracks are. There had been a large goods depot to the left of the picture, but now trains run through the site and head much deeper into the dock estate. *Paul Wright*

Above **Alexandra Dock:** A view of the site of the
station booking office on 24 September 2005.
Paul Wright

Below **Alexandra Dock:** A view looking east from
the buffer stops along the single platform in 1930.
The terminus station was provided with an overall
roof. *Stations UK*

OVER & WHARTON (1882)

Date opened:	3 July 1882
Location:	Wharton Park Road (A5018) runs through the west side of the station site
Company on opening:	London & North Western Railway
Date closed to passengers:	16 June 1947
Date closed completely:	March 1991
Company on closing:	London Midland & Scottish Railway
Present state:	Demolished – site now occupied by a housing estate
County:	Cheshire
OS Grid Ref:	SJ656665

Over & Wharton station was situated at the end of a mile-long branch line from the London & North Western Railway's premier West Coast route just to the north of Winsford, and was built to give access to the salt traffic for which Winsford was well known. The station was close to the Cheshire Lines Committee station at Winsford & Over, so to avoid confusion the LNWR opted for the Over & Wharton name.

The station was provided with one platform on the east side of the line. A timber-built single-storey building provided booking facilities, waiting rooms and staff accommodation. There were also extensive goods facilities, which is not surprising considering that the movement of freight was the line's primary purpose.

Passenger train services consisted of a shuttle that ran to Hartford station on the main

Over & Wharton: A view looking south at the buffer stops in 1950. *Stations UK*

Above **Over & Wharton:**
Looking south at the site of the
station in September 2008.
Paul Wright

line, where passengers could
connect with a variety of local
and long-distance services.

On 1 January 1917 Over
& Wharton station was
closed as a wartime economy
measure, reopening for
passenger services on 17 July
1920. In 1923 it became part
of the London Midland &
Scottish Railway, and during
the 1930s five shuttle trains
ran in each direction on
weekdays only. No trains ran
on Sundays.

Over & Wharton station
did not survive long enough
to become part of the
nationalised British Railways,
being closed by the LMS on 16
June 1947. The line remained
in use for goods services
until March 1991 after which
the track was lifted almost
immediately.

SOUTHPORT Central (1882)

Date opened:	4 September 1882
Location:	Junction of Derby Road and Kensington Road
Company on opening:	West Lancashire Railway
Date closed to passengers:	1 May 1901
Date closed completely:	Early 1970s
Company on closing:	Lancashire & Yorkshire Railway
Present state:	Demolished – site now occupied by a supermarket
County:	Lancashire (modern county of Merseyside)
OS Grid Ref:	SD343172

Southport Central opened on 4 September 1882 as the permanent terminus of the West Lancashire Railway's Southport to Preston line, which had reached a temporary terminus at Windsor Road in Southport on 10 June 1878. Train services operated to Preston.

On 1 November 1887 the Liverpool, Southport & Preston Junction Railway opened its line from Hillhouse Junction (on the CLC Aintree to Southport Lord Street line) to Southport Central, and services began to operate between Southport Central and Altcar & Hillhouse.

In July 1897 both the West Lancashire and the Liverpool, Southport & Preston Junction companies were absorbed into the Lancashire & Yorkshire Railway. The LYR had a large terminus at Southport Chapel Street and could see no sense in operating two termini

Right **Southport Central:** Looking west towards the site of the station in January 2006. The industrial buildings occupy the station approach lines, while the houses on the right backed onto the line and station. *Paul Wright*

Left **Southport Central:** The site of the station in January 2006, from the same viewpoint as the northbound 1986 picture below. *Paul Wright/ Martin Brown*

Below **Southport Central:** The station building was still standing in June 1986, more than 80 years after it had closed. *Martin Brown*

in such close proximity. On 1 May 1901 the LYR completed a remodelling of the approach lines to Central to allow trains to divert onto the Manchester to Southport line and into Southport Chapel Street station. On the same day Southport Central was closed to passengers and became a goods depot. It survived intact well into the 1970s, and today the site is occupied by a supermarket car park.

Left **Southport Central:** A close-up of the closed Central station. *Martin Brown*

Below **Southport Central:** This view shows the derelict main station building in June 1986. *Martin Brown*

HOLCOMBE BROOK (1882)

Date opened:	6 November 1882
Location:	South side of Bolton Road West just to the west of Longsight Road
Company on opening:	Bury & Tottington District Railway
Date closed to passengers:	4 May 1952
Date closed completely:	1960
Company on closing:	British Railways (London Midland Region)
Present state:	Demolished – site occupied by shops
County:	Lancashire
OS Grid Ref:	SD779151

Holcombe Brook station was located at the end of a 4-mile single-track branch from the East Lancashire Railway's Bury to Ramsbottom line, and was constructed by the Bury & Tottington District Railway between 1878 and 1882. The terminus station at Holcombe Brook opened on 6 November 1882, and was provided with a single platform and very basic passenger facilities. Adjacent to the platform was a run-round loop, and to the south of the station goods sidings were provided. A ramp provided access from street level.

From the day of opening, passenger services were operated by the Lancashire & Yorkshire Railway, with services running to Bury Bolton Street and calling at intermediate stations at Greenmount, Tottington and Woolfold.

Only a year after opening the line found itself competing against a steam tram service that opened along the Tottington Road. By 1904 the steam trams had been replaced by electric vehicles, and in response the LYR introduced a railmotor service to the line in 1905. It also opened four halts on the branch in a bid to win more passengers.

In 1913 Dick, Kerr & Co of Preston persuaded the LYR to allow it to electrify the

line for free with 3,500 volts DC overhead electrification equipment. This would allow the electrical company to market its wares. The LYR agreed and electric services, the first in the world to use high-voltage DC, began to operate. In 1916 the LYR bought the electrical equipment from Dick, Kerr, and shortly afterwards converted the overhead system to the 1,200-volt DC live rail system that it used on its Bury to Manchester line.

Amazingly for such a rural branch line, passenger services between Holcombe Brook and Bury reached a peak of 28 a day on

Above **Holcombe Brook:** A view looking north towards the site of the buffer stops in October 2008. Shops now occupy the station site. *Mark Campion*

Below **Holcombe Brook:** Looking south towards the station site; the headwall behind the van marks the end of the station, which was situated on the other side but at a lower elevation. *Mark Campion*

weekdays in 1938, the line then being part of the London Midland & Scottish Railway.

The line became part of British Railways in 1948. By 1951 the electrical equipment was worn out and in need of replacement, but BR considered that it was not worth the cost. Electric train services therefore ceased to run in 1951, and for 14 months, while closure procedures were followed, the line reverted to steam operation. Holcombe Brook station closed to passenger services on 4 May 1952, although goods services continued to operate until 1960, after which the line was cut back to Tottington.

Today nothing remains of the station, the site of which has been developed with shops.

Holcombe Brook: A view of the station in 1913, after the short-lived overhead electrification had been installed. *NRM*

SOUTHPORT Lord Street (1884)

Date opened:	1 September 1884
Location:	West side of Lord Street
Company on opening:	Cheshire Lines Committee
Date closed to passengers:	7 January 1952
Date closed completely:	7 July 1952
Company on closing:	British Railways (London Midland Region)
Present state:	Station building still exists, but platforms and trainshed have been demolished and the site is occupied by a Morrisons supermarket
County:	Lancashire (modern county of Merseyside)
OS Grid Ref:	SD332169

The grand terminus that was Southport Lord Street opened as part of the Southport & Cheshire Lines Extension Railway on 1 September 1884.

The line, which ran from Aintree Central to Southport Lord Street, was designed to give access to the lucrative holiday market at Southport as an alternative to the LYR route. From the beginning it was served by trains from Liverpool Central and from Manchester, the former following a circuitous route that could not hope to compete with the direct Liverpool Exchange to Southport Chapel Street route.

The station had a grand frontage building complete with clock tower, and five platform faces covered by a glazed overall roof. Most unusually for a terminus, a footbridge connected its platforms; situated about halfway along the platforms, it seemed to serve very little purpose, as it would be hardly likely that arriving passengers would want to change platforms

for another service when the only option was to go back in the same direction. It has been suggested that the CLC installed the bridge as it hoped that another line would come in from the north, then interchange between services would be possible. However, it seems to have been an expensive installation considering that the proposed line never even had Parliamentary approval and, as things turned out, it never did.

The station closed to passengers on 1

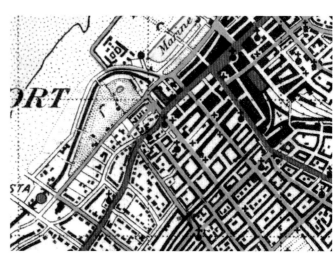

Above **Southport Lord Street:** A view looking at the buffer stops at Lord Street in 1949. The station looks very empty, for by this time during the winter months only a handful of services ran. *Stations UK*

Right **Southport Lord Street:** The clock tower in December 2005. *Paul Wright*

January 1917 as a wartime economy measure, reopening on 1 April 1919.

The Southport & Cheshire Lines Extension Railway never really delivered the traffic levels that the CLC had hoped for. In 1940, during the Second World War, the line did see intensive use for a period when the former LYR Southport to Liverpool line was damaged by enemy bombing close to Liverpool Exchange station. The damage was such that the line was out of use for several weeks, so a number of specials were run from Liverpool Central to Southport Lord Street.

C.L.C. This ticket is not transferable, and is issued subject to the Bye-Laws, Regulations and Conditions stated in the Committee's Time Tables. AVAILABLE ON DAY OF ISSUE ONLY
Southport (Lord St.)
TO
KNOTTY ASH & Stanley
First Class   Knotty Ash   Fare 2s

0363

SEP26.1.03

1 2 3 4 5 6
CHESHIRE LINES COMMITTEE. (B)
SOUTHPORT (LORD STREET)
Admit ONE to Platform. Charge 1d.
This ticket must be given up on leaving Platform. Available ONE HOUR.
FOR CONDITIONS SEE BACK.
7 8 9 10 11 12
Prohibited from entering trains

4660

15AP30

Left **Southport Lord Street:** The station frontage seen from Lord Street in December 2005. *Paul Wright*

Below **Southport Lord Street:** A close up view of the clock tower and the original Southport & Cheshire Lines Extension Railway initials 'etched in stone'. *Paul Wright*

The CLC became part of British Railways in 1948 and shortly afterwards the platforms at Southport Lord Street were extended so that longer trains could be accommodated. However, within a couple of years the line was to close. It was decided that long-distance trains could be diverted to use Southport Chapel Street and that the Southport & Cheshire Lines Extension Railway could close in its entirety. Lord Street station closed to passenger services on 7 January 1952 and to goods six months later.

This was not the end of the station's life as a transport hub, however, as it became Southport's Ribble bus station. It remained almost entirely unaltered until the late 1980s, except for the levelling of the areas between the platforms where the tracks had been. It then closed as a bus station and the trainshed was demolished. In the early 1990s a Morrisons supermarket was built on the site, but the station frontage building was restored and still stands today, complete with a plaque informing shoppers of its former use.

WEST KIRBY (1886)

Date opened:	19 April 1886
Location:	North side of Grange Road (A540)
Company on opening:	Birkenhead Joint (Great Western Railway and London & North Western Railway)
Date closed to passengers:	17 September 1956
Date closed completely:	7 May 1962
Company on closing:	British Railways (London Midland Region)
Present state:	Demolished – site now occupied by a leisure centre
County:	Cheshire (modern county of Merseyside)
OS Grid Ref:	SJ214870

West Kirby's joint station was opened on 19 April 1886 as the northern terminus station on the Great Western Railway (GWR) and London & North Western Railway's (LNWR) extension to their 1866 branch line from Hooton to Parkgate as part of their Birkenhead Joint Railway. The extension ran from Parkgate through Heswall, Thurstaston and Caldy terminating at West Kirby.

The station was only a short distance to the east of the Wirral Railway's West Kirby station, which had opened in 1878 and was extensively rebuilt as quite a grand affair in 1896.

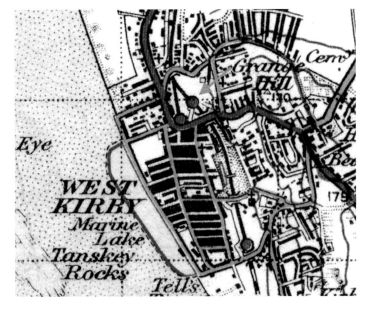

In comparison the Birkenhead Joint Railway's station was very modest. It consisted of a single platform on the west side of the line. A single-storey brick building provided passenger and parcels facilities. The Hooton to West Kirby Branch line was a single-track route but at West Kirby station a passing loop was provided as was a small turntable and watering facilities. Although the station was a terminus the line continued beyond the station to the north and made a connection with the Wirral Railway, which facilitated the movement of goods between the two networks. Also in the early days some long-distance passenger services used the connection as did excursion traffic.

From the start regular passenger services operated from West Kirby to Hooton, which was an important Junction station on the Birkenhead Joint Railway's Birkenhead Woodside to Chester line. Connections could be made at Hooton with London Paddington express trains as well as with many local and inter-regional services. During the peak times some West Kirby services continued on from Hooton and went as far as Birkenhead Woodside. For West Kirby residents travel to Birkenhead was far quicker from the Wirral Railway Company's Station.

Above **West Kirby:** A view looking north at the site of the station in October 2008. *Paul Wright*

Right **West Kirby:** A view looking south, also in October 2008. The line continued through the gap in the trees along what is now the Wirral Way. *Paul Wright*

In 1923 the London Midland & Scottish Railway (LMS) became the joint partner with the GWR but very little changed and service patterns remained constant. As the LMS had taken over the Wirral Railway consideration was given to the idea of building a new station at West Kirby that would accommodate both

lines. The plans were never realised. In 1938 the former Wirral Railway line between West Kirby and Birkenhead saw the introduction of electric train services making that route even more preferable to the joint line.

In 1948 the Hooton to West Kirby line became part of British Railways (London Midland Region). In 1950 nine trains operated in each direction on weekdays with four on a Saturday. The Hooton to West Kirby line suffered from increasing road competition in the 1950s and its passenger service was withdrawn on 17 September 1956. The very last train to leave West Kirby left for Hooton at 9.55pm. Many local people turned out to see it leave. Attached to the last train was a box van carrying two circus elephants which made a loud noise as the train pulled away from the station.

In 1961 newly introduced DMUs ran along the line to West Kirby station. However, they were not for the use of passengers. The line was being used to train drivers in the use of the DMUs.

West Kirby station continued to be used for goods until the 7th May 1962. The last goods train stopped at all of the former passenger stations and removed any remaining fixtures and fittings that were of value. Early in 1964 the demolition gangs began their work by making a break in the line at West Kirby station.

In the early 1970s the route of the Hooton-West Kirby branch was chosen to create Britain's first country park, the Wirral Country Park. The site of the lines at West Kirby's joint station did not survive and has been developed.

West Kirby: A view looking north in 1930. A train has arrived at the single platform, probably from Hooton. The engine would have run around its train ready for a return journey south. *Stations UK*

WIGAN Central (1892)

Date opened:	3 October 1892
Location:	River Way (part of the A49) runs through the site
Company on opening:	Manchester Sheffield & Lincolnshire Railway
Date closed to passengers:	2 November 1964
Date closed completely:	5 April 1965
Company on closing:	British Railways (London Midland Region)
Present state:	Demolished
County:	Lancashire (modern county of Greater Manchester)
OS Grid Ref:	SJ594057

In 1874 the Cheshire Lines Committee promoted the idea of a Wigan Junction Railway, which would run from its main Liverpool to Manchester line at Glazebrook and link it to the lucrative Lancashire coalfields. Only the Manchester Sheffield & Lincolnshire constituent of the CLC remained interested in the concept, and it was that company that built the line, opening it to goods services in 1879. Initially the line left the main line at Glazebrook by an east to north curve, which meant that services could only easily go towards Manchester. A number of passenger stations opened on the line in 1884, including Culcheth, Lowton St Mary's, Plank Lane for West Leigh (later West Leigh & Bedford), Bickershaw & Abram, Strangeways & Hindley (later Hindley South), Lower Ince, and the terminus at Wigan Darlington Street.

In 1892 a half-mile extension was opened to a new terminus at Wigan Central, which consisted of two platforms giving three platform faces, with substantial buildings and large platform canopies. At some point during

the 20th century the station was reduced to a single platform.

Initially trains ran from Wigan Central to Manchester Central, but in 1900 a west to north curve was put in at Glazebrook, which allowed trains to head to and from Liverpool. The line subsequently became part of the GCR and, in 1923, part of the LNER, but it was operated as part of the CLC system. Monday to Friday services in 1903 saw the

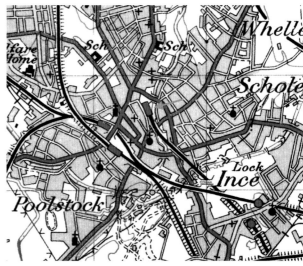

GCR run eight trains to Manchester and six to Warrington each day. Services increased under the LNER, especially during the war years. However, after 1945 the line went into decline and the last services from Wigan Central were to Irlam or Manchester Central. Latterly some of these services where operated by DMUs until the end came on 1 November 1964. The line lingered on for goods services until 1968.

Today the site of Wigan Central is occupied by a road and a shopping development.

Above **Wigan Central:** The opening day at Wigan Central station in 1892. All the people involved in building the station are lined up on the platform. *Postcard*

Below **Wigan Central:** The station's roadside building in the 1960s – it was demolished in 1973. *Postcard*

Top **Wigan Central:** A view looking north in 1951. The platform to the right was a bay, and coaches occupy the station's main platform. *Stations UK*

Above **Wigan Central:** The station is seen during a visit by a rail tour in the 1960s. *Bevan Price*

Left **Wigan Central:** The site of the station looking north in January 2006. *Paul Wright*

LIVERPOOL Riverside (1895)

Date opened:	12 June 1895
Location:	Alongside dock on the west side of Princess Parade
Company on opening:	Mersey Docks & Harbour Board
Date closed to passengers	25 February 1971
Date closed completely:	25 February 1971
Company on closing:	Mersey Docks & Harbour Board
Present state:	Demolished
County:	Lancashire modern county of Merseyside
OS Grid Ref:	SJ337906

Liverpool Riverside station was opened by the Mersey Docks & Harbour Board adjacent to its Princess Landing Stage, which was used by transatlantic liners connecting Liverpool with New York and other global destinations.

The station was located at the end of a branch line that ran through the dock estate on tramway-style lines and connected with the London & North Western Railway's Waterloo goods station. From Waterloo Goods two tunnels ascended at a very steep gradient to

Edge Hill, where connections to the main LNWR system could be made.

Riverside station had three platform faces, two of which were provided by an island platform, and an overall roof. The adjacent Princess Parade, the roadway on the west side of the station, was also covered so that passengers could proceed to the ocean liners without being exposed to the weather.

From the time of its opening Riverside station was served by boat trains. The LNWR American Specials were always treated as special arrivals at the station. Because of weight restrictions on the line to the docks, the engines that had worked the specials from Euston were detached at Edge Hill (and attached at Edge Hill in the up direction), and two 'special tanks', rebuilt as side tanks and named *Euston* and *Liverpool*, worked the trains down to Riverside. This situation persisted until 1950, when bridge strengthening in the docks allowed main-line locomotives to reach the station.

The Mersey Docks & Harbour Board had hoped that both the Lancashire & Yorkshire Railway and the Cheshire Lines Committee, which both ran boat trains to Liverpool, would use Riverside. However, due to the conditions

imposed on train movements through the docks, trains had to move at walking pace, preceded by a man with a flag, and only the LNWR and its successors ever used the station for scheduled services.

During both World Wars Riverside station was extremely busy as it was used by

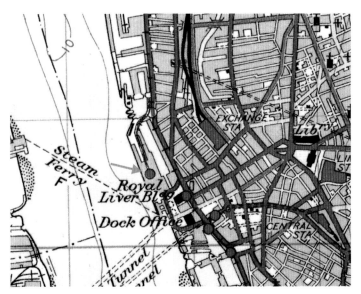

Opposite page **Liverpool Riverside:** A quiet period at Riverside in 1950: the three platform faces at the station could become incredibly busy when boat trains arrived to deposit or collect transatlantic passengers. *Stations UK*

Above **Liverpool Riverside:** The approach to Riverside in November 1988. *Michael Kaye*

troop trains from all over the country. It was closed by accident on 21 October 1949, but reopened on 27 March 1950. By the 1960s the transatlantic liner trade had declined as air travel became more popular. As a result Riverside station saw less and less use, although it was very popular during the 1960s for railtours.

The last train to use the station was on 25 February 1971; this was a troop train being run in connection with 'The Troubles' in Northern Ireland.

The station was demolished in the early 1990s and the site is now occupied by new waterfront office

accommodation. Some sections of the approach lines still survive, but it is likely that they will be built over within a few years.

Top **Liverpool Riverside:** The approach to the station in June 2005. *Paul Wright*

Centre **Liverpool Riverside:** Another view of the approach, also in June 2005. *Paul Wright*

Left **Liverpool Riverside:** The site of Riverside station in June 2005, looking north. *Paul Wright*

SEACOMBE & EGREMONT (1895)

Date opened:	1 June 1895
Location:	Church Road/Borough Road, opposite Seacombe Ferry Terminal
Company on opening:	Wirral Railway
Date closed to passengers:	4 January 1960
Date closed completely:	17 June 1963
Company on closing:	British Railways (London Midland Region)
Present state:	Demolished
County:	Cheshire (modern county of Merseyside)
OS Grid Ref:	SJ325908

The line on which the terminal station of Seacombe stood was the last addition to the Wirral Railway company's (WR) network of lines that stretched from Birkenhead to West Kirby and to New Brighton. The branch to Seacombe left the New Brighton branch at Seacombe Junction from where heavy engineering was required to drive the line through a sandstone ridge and through to the banks of the Mersey at Seacombe. There was only one other station on the line at Liscard & Poulton.

The station was located on the north side of Church Road and to the west of Borough Road close to the Seacombe Ferry terminal which offered good connections to Liverpool. Church Road curved around to the north and passed over the line at the station's western end by means of a large single-span iron bridge. At the time of opening the station was provided with two timber-built platforms that provided three platform faces. The southernmost platform was adjacent to Church Road and had a single platform face and the northernmost was an island platform. The station was accessed from Borough Road on which stood a single-storey timber building at the eastern end of the southernmost platform.

A signal box located on the north side of the line at the west end of the station, adjacent to the Church Road bridge, controlled train movements.

The reason why the station was timber-built and very basic was because the WR intended to build a more substantial station adjacent to the actual ferry terminal. The idea was never realised and Seacombe station was to remain much the same throughout its life.

When the station opened on 1 June 1895 it was served by trains that ran to West Kirby. Nineteen trains per day ran in each direction on weekdays at half-hourly intervals with nine on Sundays. Passenger numbers were high with over 2000 being carried over the first weekend of operation.

From 1897 the WR introduced a train service to New Brighton which was known locally as the 'Seacombe Dodger' but was never really very successful as it took a somewhat indirect route to the resort which lies only a few miles to the north of Seacombe by road. In 1899 it ran only during the afternoons and evenings and it was designed to cater for tourists travelling from Liverpool on the Ferry. Competition from the Wallasey Borough tramways from 1902 did not help. The service survived until 1910.

Above **Seacombe & Egremont:** In 1953 a Wrexham Central service prepares to depart from the recently reconstructed island platform at Seacombe Station. With the ending of the West Kirby service in 1938 three platform faces were no longer necessary. British Railway's decided that only the island platform needed to be upgraded and the platform on the right of the picture was taken out of use. In the background the clock tower of the Seacombe Ferry terminal from which ferries operated to Liverpool can clearly be seen.
R. M.. Casserley

On 1 May 1898 train services of the Wrexham, Mold & Connahs Quay Railway (WM&CQR) that linked Wrexham to Bidston were with the agreement of the WR extended to run through to Seacombe. By this date the WM&CQR had effectively become part of the Great Central Railway (GCR) but the situation was not formalised until 1904. The Wrexham trains proved very popular with Liverpool residents who used them to enjoy a day out in the country.

On 1 July 1901 Seacombe station was renamed as Seacombe & Egremont. By 1906 there were 13 GCR departures on weekdays from Seacombe between 07.50 and 20.55. Five of the departures went to Chester Northgate, one to Buckley Junction with the remainder serving Wrexham. The WR ran 16 trains on weekdays from Seacombe to West Kirby in 1906.

In 1923 Seacombe & Egremont station became part of the London Midland & Scottish Railway (LMS) and the former GCR train service became part of the London & North Eastern Railway (LNER). By 1929 the LMS had reduced the Seacombe to West Kirby service to one train per hour in each direction but the LNER continued to offer an extensive service to Chester Northgate and Wrexham.

In the early 1930s the LMS drew up plans for the electrification of the former WR lines between Birkenhead Park, West Kirby and New Brighton. The Seacombe branch was not considered. In 1938 the electrification was complete and it allowed passengers to travel direct between Liverpool and West Kirby as there was an end-on connection between the LMS and the under-river Mersey Railway at Birkenhead Park. This made travelling by ferry to Seacombe to connect to a West Kirby train far less attractive. Passengers could also travel from Liverpool to Bidston by train and connect directly into the LNER service. Seacombe & Egremont station suffered as a result and the West Kirby service was withdrawn on 12 March 1938.

During the early years of the Second World War Seacombe & Egremont station was used to evacuate thousands of local children to the safety of the countryside.

On 1 January 1948 Seacombe & Egremont station became part of the nationalised British Railways (London Midland Region) and from 5 January 1953 it reverted to being simply Seacombe. During the early years of the 1950s the island platform was reconstructed using concrete sections backfilled with gravel. A new entrance was provided which led directly onto the platform and the southernmost platform was taken out of use. In the late 1950s 13 trains ran from Seacombe to either Wrexham or Chester on weekdays with only three trains on a Sunday running to Wrexham only. British Railways decided to close Seacombe and Liscard & Poulton stations and divert the Wrexham and Chester trains to New Brighton. The last service left Seacombe for Wrexham on Sunday 3 January 1960 and the station closed to passenger services.

The line lingered on for a few more years as a goods line but the last services in June 1963. Much of the alignment of the Seacombe branch was used to form the Kingsway Road Tunnel that opened in 1971 but the station site itself was used for a housing development. Only a small section of sandstone wall remains today.

Above left **Seacombe & Egremont:** Looking west towards the site of the station, a small section of sandstone wall is the only surviving part. *Paul Wright*

Above right **Seacombe & Egremont:** A view looking towards the east at the site of Seacombe Station in January 2010. The view is taken from the site of the bridge which carried Church Road over the line. In the distance can be seen Liverpool which could be reached from Seacombe by Ferry. *Paul Wright*

Left **Seacombe & Egremont:** A view looking northwest along the site of the southernmost platform of Seacombe station in January 2010. The older housesin the distance on the left of the picture are on Church Road. To the right of these houses was the Church Road bridge under which trains passed on their way to Bidston. *Paul Wright*

Below **Seacombe & Egremont:** A view looking west from the 1950s built entrance at Seacombe station shortly after it had closed in 1960. Originally both of the stations platforms had been constructed out of wood but in the early 1950s the island platform was rebuilt using concrete backfilled with gravel. A new entrance was created from Borough Road at the same time. The platform to the left of the picture was taken out of use after the island platform had been reconstructed. The building on the left is the original station ticket office and waiting room. *Stations UK*

DINGLE (1896)

Date opened:	21 December 1896
Location:	Kedleston Street/Park Road
Company on opening:	Liverpool Overhead Railway
Date closed to passengers:	30 December 1956
Date closed completely:	30 December 1956
Company on closing:	British Railways (London Midland Region)
Present state:	Street-level building demolished and replaced by vehicle repair garage. Platform level still extant and in use as vehicle repair facilities.
County:	Lancashire (modern county of Merseyside)
OS Grid Ref:	SJ363876

Situated on the Liverpool Overhead Railway's Dingle extension, the station opened as the southern terminus of the line on 21 December 1896. The LOR had opened in 1893 as an elevated electric railway from Herculaneum Dock to Seaforth Sands, and the

Above **Dingle:** The site of the underground platform in 1999.
The station is now in use as a vehicle repair workshop. *Nick Catford*

Left **Dingle:** A 1999 view of the subway that led down from street level to the station platform. *Nick Catford*

Below **Dingle:** A view of the site of the street-level building in September 2005. *Paul Wright*

original line was 16 feet above street level on an iron viaduct that carried it above Liverpool's busy Dock Road and directly above the Dock Board's railway, which ran throughout the length of the dock system linking the various goods facilities.

Dingle station, however, was very different, as it was situated underground. The extension of 1896 drove the line inland from the docks and involved plunging into a tunnel that ran from the dock area to Park Road in the south Liverpool suburb of Dingle. The

Above **Dingle:** A view of the underground platform on 10 April 1955. A Seaforth & Litherland train waits to depart. *D. J. Norton*

Below **Dingle:** The street-level entrance, photographed on the same day. *D. J. Norton*

station consisted of an island platform located in a tunnel, and steps and ramps led up to a brick building on the busy Park Road, which connected Dingle with the city centre.

When the station opened frequent electric train services operated to Seaforth Sands, and from 1905 these were extended to Seaforth & Litherland station on the Lancashire & Yorkshire Railway's Liverpool-Southport line.

Dingle station was the scene of the LOR's worst disaster. In December 1901 an electrical fire on board an incoming train got out of control and, fanned by the tunnel draught, quickly engulfed the terminus. Six people died

and such was the devastation that the station was closed for more than a year.

The Liverpool Overhead Railway was a much-loved and well-used line, but it was discovered that the elevated sections of the line had corroded badly due to steam from the Dock Board Railway running beneath it. Despite local opposition, the line closed, together with all of its stations, on 30 December 1956.

Dingle station's street-level building was demolished, but its platform level found a new life as a vehicle repair workshop.

Above **Dingle:** A close-up of the station entrance, also on 10 April 1955, showing an abundance of posters advertising the line. *D. J. Norton*

ST HELENS Central 1900

Date opened:	2 January 1900
Location:	East of Birchley Street
Company on opening:	Liverpool, St Helens & South Lancashire Railway
Date closed to passengers:	1 March 1952
Date closed completely:	4 January 1965
Company on closing:	British Railways (London Midland Region)
Present state:	Demolished
County:	Lancashire (modern county of Merseyside)
OS Grid Ref:	SJ513956

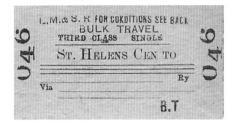

Below **St Helens Central** : An enthusiasts' special is seen at St Helens Central in September 1963. *Bevan Price*

Left **St Helens Central:** The same special approaches the station. *Bevan Price*

Below **St Helens Central:** The special prepares to depart. *Bevan Price*

The simple terminus station that was St Helens Central station was situated at the end of a branch from the Glazebrook to Wigan Central line at Lowton St Mary's. This line had been sanctioned as early as July 1885 and the original intention was to create a line that would link Wigan to Southport by creating a route from Lowton St Mary's to Fazakerley Junction on the CLC's North Liverpool Extension line.

The railway company that was formed to build the line, the St Helens & Wigan Junction Railway (which became the Liverpool, St Helens & South Lancashire Railway on 26 July 1889) was in constant financial difficulty and, despite the first sod being cut on 28 January 1888, it did not open to goods traffic until 1 July 1895, and then only to St Helens. It was to take another five years for the line to be brought up to passenger standards, by which

Left **St Helens Central:** The site of the station booking office, looking north in February 2006.
Bevan Price

Below **St Helens Central:** A view looking north from the buffer stops in 1922. The station was only ever supposed to be a temporary structure, but it remained unaltered until closure.
Stations UK

time any hope of continuing west had been abandoned.

The line remained a minor branch that was of far more use for goods as it was linked to a number of collieries in the Lancashire coalfield. Passenger services were always secondary. In 1906 the line became part of the GCR, then the LNER in 1923.

The station was on top of an embankment and was a simple single platform with a waiting shelter; the ticket office was at street level. It did not survive long into the nationalisation era, closing on 1 March 1952. Today the name St Helens Central lives on as the town's Shaw Street station was renamed Central in the 1980s – long enough after the closure of the original Central to avoid any confusion.

MANCHESTER Mayfield (1910)

Date opened:	8 August 1910
Location:	South side of Fairfield adjacent to Manchester London Road/Piccadilly station
Company on opening:	London & North Western Railway
Date closed to passengers:	23 August 1960
Date closed completely:	Unknown
Company on closing:	British Railways (London Midland Region)
Present state:	Station is still extant and unused with trainshed intact. The roadside building was gutted by fire in the summer of 2005.
County:	Lancashire (modern county of Merseyside)
OS Grid Ref:	SJ851977

The London & North Western Railway's busiest station in Manchester was London Road, and by the first decade of the 20th century it had become so busy that it could hardly cope with the levels of traffic being carried. In particular the LNWR had great difficulty accommodating both main-line long-distance trains and local suburban services.

The answer was to build a new station to the south of Manchester London Road, and this new station opened as Manchester Mayfield on 8 August 1910. In effect it was really an overspill station for Manchester London Road (renamed Piccadilly in 1960). It was

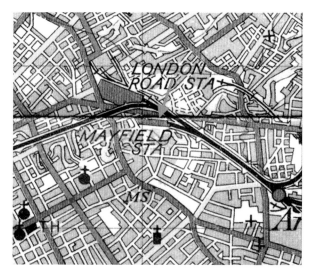

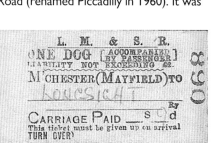

Above **Manchester Mayfield:** A view looking west into the station in August 2004. *Paul Sutcliffe*

Below **Manchester Mayfield:** A view from track level looking towards the buffers in August 2004. *Paul Sutcliffe*

Above **Manchester Mayfield:** A view looking out towards the platforms from the concourse, also in August 2004. *Paul Sutcliffe*

Below **Manchester Mayfield:** The station concourse in August 2004. *Paul Sutcliffe*

situated above street level, the lines leading into it coming off a brick viaduct. It was built of red brick and had an imposing two-storey frontage building that provided access from street level. Three platforms were provided, giving five platform faces, two of the platforms being islands. On the north side of the station a ramp led up from street level, allowing vehicular access to the platforms. An overall roof supported on iron columns was provided, covering all the platforms. A footbridge connected Mayfield with London Road station to help passengers who needed to change trains. Train services from the station operated to various destinations on the Buxton, Crewe and Macclesfield lines.

Mayfield Station became part of the London Midland Scottish Railway (LMS) in 1923 and that companies 18th July 1932 to the 11th September 1932 Summer timetable shows thirteen weekday departures from the station which called at all stations to Stockport. The weekday services ran mostly in the morning and evening rush hour. The situation seems to have altered on Saturday's as more Stockport services appear to have operated

from Mayfield throughout the daytime period. It is possible that this would have been because there would have been numerous holiday specials running from Manchester London Road on Saturday's. The same 1932 timetable also shows a number of long distance arrival's used Mayfield Station For many years it served Manchester's commuters well, but following electrification of many of the local lines in 1960 the station closed on 23 August of that year. It lay derelict for nearly a decade but was eventually converted into a parcels depot, opening on 6 July 1970.

The parcels depot closed in the late 1980s and since then the station has stood idle. The derelict interior was used in the television drama *Prime Suspect 5* as a drug dealer's haunt.

As Manchester Piccadilly station (formerly London Road) is once again running out of capacity, there has been a proposal to reopen Mayfield. This will either be as a terminus, as it was before, or the lines will be extended through the station to join up with the existing line to Oxford Road.

Below **Manchester Mayfield:** A view looking east away from the buffer stops within the trainshed in August 1957. *S. J. Hemington, Manchester Libraries*

Above **Manchester Mayfield:** A view looking east at the front of the station in January 2010. In recent years the building has been damaged by fire and despite suggestions that it could re-open to passenger trains in order to ease congestion at nearby Manchester Piccadilly it continues to deteriorate. *Mark Aldred*

Below **Manchester Mayfield:** A view looking towards the northwest along the derelict platforms at the station in January 2010. The electrified lines on the right of the picture lead into Manchester Piccadilly station. *Mark Aldred*

GLADSTONE DOCK (1914)

Date opened:	7 September 1914
Location:	West of Rimrose Road in the MD&HB's dock estate
Company on opening:	Lancashire & Yorkshire Railway
Date closed to passengers:	7 July 1924
Date closed completely:	7 July 1924
Company on closing:	London Midland & Scottish Railway
Present state:	Demolished – no evidence of the station or railway remains
County:	Lancashire
OS Grid Ref:	SJ329962

Gladstone Dock station was located on the North Mersey branch, which ran from Fazakerley Junction, on the Liverpool Exchange to Wigan line. The line was opened in August 1867 as an important goods line linking the north Liverpool Docks with the LYR route to the east. Connections to the Ormskirk-Liverpool line were provided at Sefton Junction (Aintree), going from west to north, and at North Mersey Branch Junction, from south to east.

In 1906 the LYR electrified the North Mersey branch from North Mersey Branch Junction to Sefton Junction and opened two

Gladstone Dock: A view of the station in 1914, showing the simple facilities that were provided. *NRM*

stations, at Ford and Linacre Road. They were served by an electric commuter service that ran from Aintree Sefton Arms station to Liverpool Exchange.

On 7 September 1914 the LYR extended the electrification to a new station at Gladstone Dock, located on a viaduct and consisting of just a single platform. The service on this section of the line lasted less than 10 years, ending on 7 July 1924.

The line through the site of Gladstone Dock station remained open for goods services until the late 1960s. Today the site of the station is inside the extensive Mersey Dock estate, but no evidence of it remains.

Above **Gladstone Dock:** Looking south-west towards the site of Gladstone Dock and Seaforth Sands stations in June 2005. Gladstone Dock was on an embankment. *Paul Wright*

Since its launch in 2004, *Subterranea Britannica's* *DISUSED STATIONS* web site has become established as one of the most comprehensive online photographic records of closed stations in the UK with a wide selection of 'then' and 'now' photographs.

Each station page includes a selection of archive pictures showing the station before closure and the site as it appears today plus ordnance survey maps, tickets, timetables and a brief history of the station or line.

With over 6000 closed station in the UK this will be a very long term project but with 1421 stations covered (as of June 2010) we have already made a serious dent in that number but there is still a long way to go.

Disused Stations welcomes contributions from anyone, any station, any line, any period in time but if you aren't the photographer please make sure you have the copyright owner's permission before sending photographs for inclusion on the web site.

Visit us at www.disused-stations.org.uk/sites.shtml
- you won't be disappointed.